D1609941

Injured Pride

Injured Pride

The Lions in South Africa

Carwyn James
and **Chris Rea**

Edited by Rupert Cherry

Arthur Barker Limited   London
A subsidiary of Weidenfeld (Publishers) Limited

Published in Great Britain by
Arthur Barker Limited 91 Clapham High Street
London SW4 7TA

ISBN 0 213 16782 4

Printed in Great Britain by
Butler & Tanner Ltd, Frome and London

Contents

Illustrations

7,000 Miles in South Africa

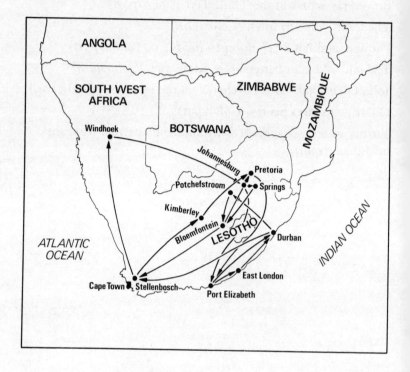

This map shows the journeys the Lions had to make after landing at Johannesburg on Sunday 4 May. They trained at Vanderbijlpark 15 miles away for four days, and then flew to Port Elizabeth for their first match. Their journey continued up to East London and Durban, then across to Potchefstroom and down to Bloemfontein. After that 600 miles down to Cape Town for the match at Stellenbosch and the First Test. Then 800 miles up to Windhoek, and another 800 miles across to Johannesburg. Springs was only 30 miles away, but then they had to go down to Bloemfontein for the Second Test, back up again to Pretoria, and a 600-mile trip to Port Elizabeth for the Third Test. After that they travelled 500 miles up to Durban, and 800 miles down to Cape Town. Finally they went up to Kimberley and Pretoria for the last Test, a total of more than 7,000 miles.

1
Sport and Politics

At the beginning of the 1979–80 Rugby season in the British Isles the chances of the Lions being sent to tour South Africa in 1980 were about as remote as England's hopes of winning the grand slam in the early part of 1980. That both events actually happened was one of the most astounding doubles that has ever occurred in the history of Rugby Football. Political agitators, who had nothing to do with sport at all, had so influenced some people's minds, and particularly the minds of those who had political power, that in 1978 Scotland called off their tour to South Africa. No invitation was issued to South Africa to make the scheduled tour to Britain in 1978–9, and Australia were prevented by their own government from going to South Africa in 1979.

Politics was being brought into sport, into amateur sport, and by some curiously twisted thinking Rugby Football was being linked with the Olympic Games which were due to be held in Moscow in 1980. In the early part of 1979 even men prominent in the hierarchy of Rugby administration were saying that a British Lions team could not possibly be sent to South Africa the following year because it would mean the banning of British athletes from the Olympic Games in Moscow.

Few people care for the policy of apartheid which has prevailed in South Africa, but most ordinary level-headed sportsmen, and women, are too engrossed in their particular pastime to bother about the political thinking of their opponents, even if those opponents have any deep thoughts politically, which in the majority of cases they have not. Until Russia invaded Afghanistan it could be said that because an Englishman wanted to run in

Moscow it did not necessarily mean that he agreed with, or condoned, the type of government under which the people in the United Soviet Socialist Republic have to live. Neither did it mean that because a man played Rugby against South Africa that he agreed with, or condoned, apartheid. However, politicians, and political agitators, had forced their way into sport, and in 1979 had even succeeded in frightening a few people in Rugby Football. Not every administrator in the game had the courage and clear thinking of the late Sir William Ramsay, who a decade earlier had rebuffed and rebuked the politicians who tried to interfere. Still in spite of a faint heart here and there, the International Board, composed of two representatives each from England, Scotland, Ireland, Wales, Australia, New Zealand, South Africa, and France, at their meeting in 1979, kept the 1980 tour in their schedule.

That was in March. Normally the Four Home Unions Tours Committee (England, Scotland, Ireland and Wales) would then have set about finding a manager and assistant manager for the tour. But they did not do so. Mickey Steele-Bodger of England, the chairman, a very experienced administrator who had been president of the Rugby Football Union in 1973–4, told us that they thought it would not be right to ask anyone if they were available for the tour when at that time there was such a considerable doubt whether the tour would be made. Some candidates might have to ask their employers for the promise of time off to be given on a conditional basis. Carwyn James did not agree with the delay, as he explains later, but there had been hopeful signs in South Africa that something was being done to eliminate, or at least reduce, apartheid in Rugby Football. Early in 1977 Dr Danie Craven, one of the greatest South Africans the world of Rugby Football has ever known, had come to England especially to talk to the British Press to try to convince them that the blacks and the coloureds were playing with the whites in South Africa, and that integration was going ahead rapidly throughout the game. He did not achieve the success he had hoped for, because it was the South Africans' 1978–9 tour to Britain that he was trying to save. As

President of the South African Rugby Board, his words ought to have carried more weight.

Still he did no harm, and more importantly later that year, and in 1978, some members of the Four Home Unions Committee had visited South Africa to see for themselves. During 1979 a number of British teams toured South Africa. It seemed that every Rugby man wanted to play there. Middlesex, who were English county champions, Surrey, North West Counties, Llanelli, Cardiff, and Newport were among the top sides who went. Of course they all reported back on the state of South African Rugby in regard to the apartheid question, and they all said the same thing. South Africa had gone a long way towards fulfilling the demands of the politically-minded. These reports, and their own observation, made a great impression on the Four Home Unions Committee.

So much so that towards the end of the summer they decided to invite a team of South African Barbarians to Britain and Ireland. They particularly wanted blacks and coloureds to be seen playing with whites in the British Isles. For that reason the team could not be selected on merit, because few blacks or coloureds would have been good enough. It was of course an invitation side, and it was decided to have eight whites, eight blacks, and eight coloureds in the party, none of whom had been selected for the Springbok side to tour France. That was a tour which was cancelled by the intervention of the French Government. Inevitably there was a storm of protest from the political side about the South African Barbarians' tour. The anti-apartheid campaigners said it would certainly lead to Britain being barred from the Olympic Games, and they would demonstrate, as they had done against the Springboks in 1969. They said the very make-up of the tour party was cosmetic and racialist. As usual they were very bitter.

The British Government did not like it either. Whether Mrs Thatcher, the Prime Minister, sought the advice of her husband Denis or not, we do not know, but it would surely have been a good thing if she had. Denis, at one time a well-known Rugby referee, and still an office bearer in the Middlesex County Rugby

Football Union, might at least have put the Rugby man's point of view, which her Minister of Sport, Hector Munro, former President of the Scottish Rugby Union, apparently did not. It was he who requested the Four Home Unions to cancel the Barbarians' tour. At that time the Government were busy conducting the talks on Zimbabwe-Rhodesia, and, rightly or wrongly, they thought this tour might have some adverse effect upon those talks. Some of the notions that got into politicians' heads were so far-fetched they were difficult to believe. The main reason why the government did not want the tour though was because, when she went to the Lusaka Commonwealth Conference, Mrs Thatcher had said she would uphold the Gleneagles agreement of the Commonwealth countries in 1977 which undertook to discourage sporting contact with South Africa.

Dawie de Villiers, that splendid little scrum-half who led the 1969 Springboks to Britain, and who is now the South African ambassador in London, was told that the government still stood by that agreement in spite of what had happened since. The Four Home Unions Committee said a lot had happened since, and resolutely refused to cancel the tour.

Still the protests were made. Chris de Braglio, secretary of the South African Non-Racial Olympic Committee, said Britain should be banned from the Games; indeed this tour would spell the end of the Games, and Russia let it be known that they would rather be without Britain at the Games than have a large number of black African states withdraw. Even the South African Government tried to persuade Dr Craven to stop the tour. In the world of Rugby though everyone wanted to see the Barbarians, and if there were to be any demonstrations there would be no lack of volunteers for stewards to shoo them off. The Barbarians played seven matches, three in England, two in Scotland, and two in Wales.

When the itinerary was being arranged the Scots took great care that there would be no match at Hector Munro's club, Langholm. In fact the tourists were managed by a Scottish international, Chick Henderson, who won nine caps for Scotland in the 1950s. He is a South African and had lived most of his life in South Africa, but it was a tremendous treat for him to renew acquaintance with his old friends in England as well as in Scotland. He had played for Coventry, and the Barbarians had a match there. That turned out to be the only place at which there was any evidence of organised demonstration, and it certainly was the one place where they would know how to deal with it. There were no matches in Ireland because the Irish Government prevented the tourists from going there. That was Ireland's loss; the tourists played delightful Rugby. They won four, drew one, and lost two of their matches. One of the outstanding players was the fly-half Errol Tobias, who had toured Britain previously in 1971 with the Proteas. He was only nineteen then. This time he was a player to take the eye, possibly the best black player produced by South Africa so far. There were also Rob Louw, the Western Province flank forward, who later gained selection for the Springboks' matches against South America, and against the Lions, and a grand lock forward, de Villiers Visser, to be admired.

Most important of all, though, the tour was a success from every point of view, the players were good tourists, and the integration of colours was perfect. Chick Henderson did not bother to conceal his delight at this success. 'I sincerely believe,' he said, 'that this tour has demonstrated the progress that has been made towards achieving integration in South African Rugby, and that it will open many doors.'

The doors certainly began to open. The Scottish Rugby Union and the Irish Rugby Football Union were unanimous in their decisions to proceed with the Lions tour. In the first week of January the Welsh Rugby Union met to discuss the subject. They decided in favour of the Lions tour by only 13 votes to 12. If the tour was to go ahead, though, the decision of the Four Home Unions Committee had to be unanimous. The Rugby Football Union had yet to decide. They met the day after the Welshmen had debated. In the morning they had received a letter from Hector Munro reiterating the government's view. On that same day too, the Sports Council, a body appointed by the government, met under the chairmanship of Dickie Jeeps, a former captain of England, a former British Lion, and a former president of the Rugby Football Union, to hear plans for a fact-finding mission to South Africa.

Jeeps apparently hoped that the Four Home Unions would hold up their decision until the Council had published a report on their findings. The Council had decided the previous October to send this mission to appraise the current situation, and the organization of and participation in sport in South Africa, with particular reference to major sports. But the Rugby Football Union and their former president were by now far apart on this subject. The Rugby Football Union decided by a large majority to recommend that the British Lions should tour South Africa. Nearly all the doubting Thomases had been won over by the successful demonstration of the South African Barbarians.

Three days later the Four Home Unions Committee met to ratify the decision taken by each Union that the Lions tour should go on. Again there was violent reaction. The British Olympic Association feared that Britain might be banned from competing in Moscow. How ironically events were to twist this expression of opinion!

Russia's invasion of Afganistan turned everything topsy-turvy. Politically the Lions tour was almost forgotten, as public thought was switched to the question of whether British athletes should compete in Moscow. The politicians looked away from Rugby Football, and thankfully and quietly, the Four Home Unions set about the business of preparing for the tour.

The row was by no means over, though. With a nice sense of timing the Sports Council published the findings of their mission to South Africa on the day before the Lions were due to play a mixed side of blacks and whites, the South Africa Rugby Association, in East London. The Association had invited eight white players to make up their team in order to strengthen it. To the surprise of many, the Council recommended by an overwhelming majority of 32–2 that every major international sports body in the world, including the International Olympic Committee, should reconsider its attitude towards South African sport. It called upon world sport to take note of the evidence of changes that had taken place in that country, and to go to South Africa to see for themselves. Not surprisingly some people were outraged, including Paul Stephenson, the only black member of the Sports Council, who said the Council was embarking on a terrible folly. Mr Sam Ramsammy, chairman of the South African Non-Racial Olympic Committee, described it as 'massively naive'.

For Rugby men it might have been seen as a vindication of their decision to tour, although the report made it clear that Rugby was a long way behind cricket and athletics in achieving full integration. In South Africa the report was received with 'cautious optimism'.

At the end of May, just before the first Test, Paul Stephenson again raised his voice. There had been riots in Cape Town where the Test was to be played and two coloured children had been shot and killed by the police. While Stephenson in England was asking Mickey Steele-Bodger, chairman of the Four Unions Tours Committee, to recall the Lions from South Africa, Peter Fourier, a vigorous campaigner in South Africa against apartheid, wrote to each member of the Lions party asking them to go home. They were not welcome in South Africa in the light of events in Cape Town, he said.

The players saw none of the riots, and most of them were convinced that their presence in the country did more good than harm. Punt Janson, the South African Minister of Sport, was quick to say that the Lions' visit had nothing to do with the unrest, and he did not believe the tour was responsible for any increase in incidents. Syd Millar, the Lions' manager, said they had no plans to come home, and in England Wing Commander John Lawrence, secretary of the Four Home Unions Tours Committee, said they would only consider Stephenson's request if Millar made a firm recommendation that they should return. Of course he did not do so, and except for the fact that the subject was mentioned in Parliament, the argument subsided for a time.

There was another outburst in June. This was sparked off by

an English journalist, Ian Todd, the Rugby correspondent of the *Sun*. On 18 June he wrote an article which was printed on the front page of his newspaper in which he said that the Lions had been lured to South Africa to help foster the development of multi-racial Rugby when in fact all the South African Rugby Board wanted was revenge for their defeat in 1974. That was why they had loaded teams who were supposed to be black and coloured sides with top white players. The Lions, he wrote, had been 'conned' and could not wait to get home. Some of the Lions were asking 'Why did we ever come?'

One or two other journalists wrote in somewhat similar vein, and Willie John McBride, that great Irishman who had led the 1974 Lions, was moved to say that he thought the Lions of 1980 should come home. It was not a very helpful statement from a man who was 6,000 miles away, whatever the height of his reputation in Rugby.

The South African Press gave full coverage to this theme, and there were stories of unrest within the Lions party, that half of them wanted to go home, that events in South Africa the previous week – riots in Soweto, killings in the Cape – had been too much for them, and the allegations that there had been little or no integration in the Rugby had distressed them. McBride's remarks were quoted on the front pages, and so the Lions' manager held a team meeting to take a poll of the players' opinions. It showed that none of them had said they wanted to go home. Some obviously had their own private opinions which they would keep to themselves until they got home, but none was unhappy enough to want to go home at that moment. They were not disillusioned, nor did they feel they had been 'conned'. John Mason, the Chief Rugby Correspondent of *The Daily Telegraph*, wrote, 'The tour has not turned sour; not even in defeat. Millar has insisted that the tour party is a united happy band off the field, that the players are relaxed and enjoying themselves. Millar is right. The path to honour and decency – and change – requires a helpful hand. The Lions are doing exactly that. I hope Ireland will continue this good work here next summer on a short tour, and that a variety of invited sides, major and minor, will also do so in the run-up to the Lions tour of 1986. By then there will be Spring-boks of every race and colour.'

No doubt these articles partly inspired the BBC to put on a television programme on sport and politics in which they talked not only about the Lions tour, but also on the controversy raging about whether or not British athletes should go to Moscow. From a Rugby point of view the programme achieved nothing, mainly because the one man they needed to speak on the programme, Dr Danie Craven, was not on it. Wing Commander John Lawrence, who had just returned from a fortnight following the tour said that all the black and coloured people he had spoken to were glad the Lions had made the tour, to which Paul Stephenson rather brashly retorted, 'He's talking out of the back of his neck'. Ian Todd, speaking from South Africa, reiterated the theme of his article in the *Sun*, and that was about all the programme amounted to.

2

The Choice

by Carwyn James

The first preparation for the tour was to appoint a manager and an assistant manager, or coach, as he has been styled in recent years. There was not much time, and that was the Four Home Unions Tours Committee's own fault. They should have played the Rugby game and not the political game. They should have adopted the normal procedure that has existed for several tours now of appointing the management during the summer in the year before the tour. Certainly they could not decide then whether the tour should actually take place, but they should have got on with the appointments.

As they had left it until half-way through the Rugby season in the British Isles they could not follow the normal procedure, and in fact had to do the job by invitation. The normal procedure is that in May of the the year previous to the tour the committee ask for nominations for manager and assistant manager from each of the respective Home Unions. For the 1971 Lions tour to New Zealand there were four or five nominations for manager and likewise for the assistant manager. They were interviewed at the East India Sports Club in London, and by the first week in June of 1971 we were notified that Doug Smith was to be manager, and I was the assistant manager.

That was fine because we had all the rest of the summer to prepare, and when September came, the selectors, one from each country, had four months to look around before the international season began. We could watch players even before they had been chosen to play for their countries, and that is the best time of all to see them. More especially this early start was valuable because in about October or November the Lions' itinerary was planned and you have the choice of readjusting fixtures. It had become a comfortable leisurely exercise.

The procedure for the 1980 tour put a great strain upon the management, and I would have thought on the selectors as well. In these days when international matches are doubled up on the same day it is most difficult for selectors to see all the players they need to see. In fact selection of management and players was a hurried job, and it need not have been so.

However, I thoroughly approved of the choice of Syd Millar as manager and Noel Murphy as assistant manager or coach. Millar was a unanimous choice of the Home Unions, and it was a good thing they had such an outstanding candidate because there was no time for interviews.

I understand that on future occasions the interviewing method will be reverted to, but in addition to the individual Unions' nominations, it will be possible for the Home Unions Committee themselves to put up candidates. It will be a much wider choice.

Millar's appointment though was a foregone conclusion. It would be difficult to find anyone with more or better experience for the job. Millar, now forty-five years of age, had played thirty-seven times for Ireland, had toured with the British Lions three times as a player, had coached Ireland between 1972 and 1975, and most important of all he had coached the 1974 Lions in South Africa, when they were unbeaten in that country for the first time. Although he had had so much coaching experience he was still not so far away from his playing days. His last game was for his club, Ballymena, in May 1972.

Millar was known to the world as one of the great prop forwards, but he began as a scrum-half, then as outside-half, and centre. By the time he was sixteen and an apprentice navigating officer at Belfast Nautical College he was a wing forward in Ballymena's second XV. After four years at sea he returned to play in the second row for the first XV. Then he moved up to the front row, played for Ulster, and got into the Ireland side in 1958.

So there were few positions on the field about which he had no first-hand knowledge. He had played with some of the greatest players too, spanning the years from Jackie Kyle to Barry John at outside-half, and he had propped hookers like Bryn Meredith, Ronnie Dawson, and Ken Kennedy. He had been in the same Lions sides with Tony O'Reilly and Jeff Butterfield. He had faced Wilson Whineray and Colin Meads. Millar had seen the changes in Lions' preparation and thinking that brought about the successes of 1971 in New Zealand and 1974 in South Africa. If ever a man knew the game from 'A to Z' it was Syd Millar. He is not only an astute technical analyst but a great communicator to the players, a big broad-shouldered genial man, six-feet tall, and with the build that made him weigh sixteen stones in his playing days.

Noel Murphy, a fellow Irishman, was a wing forward for Cork Constitution in the 1950s and 1960s. He won forty-one caps for Ireland and toured New Zealand twice with the Lions. He had had great success as a coach of the Irish side for two years. Under his guidance they won two Tests in Australia in the summer of 1979, as well as achieving a rare victory over Wales during the 1980 international season.

In addition to the management, 'Budge' Rogers of England, Alec Harper of Scotland, Kevin Flynn of Ireland, and Keith Rowlands of Wales were appointed as selectors of the Lions party. Of these only Harper was not a national selector for his country, but he had been a Lions selector in 1977. Rogers stipulated that he should remain with the England sides during the period of selection, which was natural because he was chairman of the England selectors.

So the search for the Lions began at Cardiff, where Wales were playing France. On the same day England took on Ireland at Twickenham. Had I been asked to predict the results of these two matches I would have gone for France and Ireland. I thought France would be very good after their tour in New Zealand, and I also felt that since Ireland had played well in Australia, one had every reason to believe that the Irish team would be a strong one. But the international season began in a strange way. France were not at all good. It was not a particularly great Welsh team, but they saw the French off fairly easily. One feels also that the Irish probably made mistakes of selection in their side against England. Their pack was annihilated. They had second thoughts later and only really came good towards the end of the season. They certainly gave a very good performance against Wales.

One thing to emerge from the Wales *v* France game was the complaint afterwards from the French about illegal use of the boot by some of the Welsh players, and in fact the spotlight fell on Paul Ringer, the Welsh flank forward. This was to have an important bearing on the next match when England played Wales at Twickenham. There was evidence that one or two French players had been hurt. Their captain Jean-Pierre Rives had received the boot and was concussed. In fact he did not play at all well for the rest of the game. It must be said though that Rives in 1980 was not the same player than he had been. He had a new job and was doing a great deal of travelling, and found the pressure on being captain a bit too much for him. But I do not wish to minimize the fact that he was injured in that match, and that the injury was unnecessary.

Then there was Paco lying on the ground, and one wondered whether the injury was deliberate or not. I looked at the video a number of times and came to the conclusion that it was not deliberate, but still he had been hit on the head by a boot, although I think it was not the boot of Paul Ringer.

I suppose it was rather natural that a great deal was written in the Press during the fortnight leading up to the England *v* Wales match at Twickenham. The new BBC News programme made a point of showing violence and attacking Paul Ringer. So in a way he was set up for the Twickenham match. I think the first half-hour of that match was an absolute disaster. It showed Rugby Football at its very worst. Nothing could have been more repugnant. The referee, David Burnett of Ireland, having warned all the players, sent Ringer off for a late tackle on John Horton. Of course there are pros and cons about the incident; some said it was deliberate, and others said it was not, but Ringer got his marching orders and was suspended by a disciplinary committee for two months. It must have seemed like a life sentence to him, because he was not picked by Wales to go to North America in May and he was not considered for the Lions tour. So that tackle probably cost him his career. (Of course there are many who would argue that to take a player like Ringer, who is not unknown for the use of the boot, is not the best possible thing for a tour. Probably the reason why Geoff Wheel did not find a place on the tour is because he has a reputation as not being the best tourist.)

In regard to the England *v* Wales match I must make the point that Wales scored two tries and England did not score any. In fact England did not look a good side. Although they were playing against 14 men for almost all the match they did things wrong tactically, and they also lacked leadership. Still, I agree they had played two and won two, and looked about to destroy some early season predictions. Before the season had started, 'Budge' Rogers had said he believed England would win three of their four matches. He thought they would lose against France in Paris. Apart from the game against Scotland though the French match turned out to be England's greatest day.

In fact England did very well for about threequarters of the match in Paris, but again I was disappointed. They could have lost even in the last ten minutes. Whether it was leadership or not I am not sure, but they brought the French back into the game, and I felt that against the odds France might well have won. No, England were still unconvincing. They had played well against Ireland, they did not play well against Wales, and played well for only threequarters of the game against France.

They had a brilliant match against Scotland, but after all, let us be honest about it, this was a poorish Scottish side. So looking at the season in general I felt there was a levelling, but sadly not a levelling up; it was a levelling down. England just about got away with it, winning the triple crown and the grand slam. It was the other leg of that historic and most remarkable double of 1980, but I do not think it would have happened in a normal year.

The selection of the Lions was made the day after England had won the grand slam, and obviously England's success would play an important part. Overall I thought the selectors did quite a good job, remembering that, as ever, there was a number of players unavailable. Ringer of course was out, and Fergus Slattery, Tony Neary, Roger Uttley, David Leslie, Steve Fenwick, and Tony Bond were not available. So you must consider that a quarter, or even a third, of the probable party could not be chosen. That made the selectors' task very difficult, more especially because they had not had the opportunity – the time being so short – to look at many players.

I think it is always a bonus to find two or three players who have not been capped by their countries, and naturally a selector looks for these. Possibly there were not any around, except Gareth Williams, not capped by Wales, who was called to South Africa to replace the injured Stuart Lane.

Another factor with which the selectors had to contend was the number of players injured. Alastair Hignell, I suppose, could be put into this category; at any rate he had not played for England during the season. I think the Lions badly needed a man like Hignell. I would certainly have put him in as my first choice full-back, and he could have been a third scrum-half because he plays equally well in both positions. He ought to have been a key choice. Another key choice, I thought, ought to have been Gordon Brown. I know he had not played for Scotland during the season, and he had not played a great deal of club Rugby, but the rest from it might well have done him good. There was no question about fitness, because once you go on tour, even the most unfit can get fit even if it takes two or three weeks. We saw that on this tour, for a very unfit Alan Tomes looked quite good after only about ten days. I would have brought Gordon Brown, and I might well have made him the elder statesman. I have already mentioned Geoff Wheel, but I think they might have found a place for him. The locks were not all that good, and Wheel would have been a far better prospect than Tomes on this tour. Michael Gibson, the Irish No. 8, was another on the injured list.

Peter Squires, the former England wing, would have been an excellent choice for South Africa. I did not think the wings available were particularly strong, except for Andy Irvine, and in fact he had to cry off just before the tour started because he had aggravated a hamstring injury which he had received while playing in a seven-a-side tournament in Hong Kong at Easter. He was replaced by Elgan Rees, who had not had a happy season at all, and had been chosen to go with Wales to North America only as a replacement. He was handily placed in another Heathrow hotel near the Lions the day before the tour was to leave, and simply changed hotels, but to me it was incredible that he should be chosen. Irvine's absence meant that they had lost one of their finest counter-attacking players, and of course the option of using him at full-back. Most important of all it meant that the Lions had to do without one of their principal place-kickers. As it turned out Irvine was able to join the tour later as a replacement when injuries had made the wing position very serious.

Ironically, at about the time Irvine flew out to South Africa, Squires was badly injured while on tour with Public Schools Wanderers in Zimbabwe. Syd Millar, hearing that Squires was in Africa, sent him an urgent message: 'Whatever you do, don't get hurt.' The Lions simply had not got a recognized wing available for the second Test. But poor Squires was caught at the bottom of a maul in practice and his left elbow was dislocated.

There was some criticism, I know, of the choice of Ray Gravell in the centre because he did not fit in with the pattern of the other three selected who were out-and-out running centres. I remember talking to Noel Murphy when he came to see Pontypridd play Llanelli in a cup match. He told me he was looking for a man to do the kind of job Steve Fenwick did, because Fenwick was not available. He wanted a sort of sweeper-upper, a good strong tackler in midfield, and when necessary a person who could set up the crash ball. The obvious choice was Ray Gravell of Llanelli who had 18 caps for Wales, but was on the bench during the 1980 season. Noel seemed to be keen on having this strong type of player – an Ian MacRae or Joggie Jansen – and in the very first match Gravell did this job against one of the hard men of the Eastern Province side. Possibly you may need a hard man, particularly for the provincial matches. Whether he gets into the Test side depends upon the kind of game the Lions want to play. I would have preferred them to play the extended game with the touch players in midfield rather than the crash ball expert.

I think the pack, although it contained several players who had been on the tour to New Zealand in 1977, looked unlikely to match the one produced by Syd Millar in 1974. That pack, I suppose, was the finest ever seen in South Africa, and certainly stronger than the 1971 pack in New Zealand. Probably the 1974 forwards were the strongest ever to represent the British Lions.

The choice of Bill Beaumont as captain of the team was almost inevitable in view of England's success and the unavailability of other candidates. But this 1980 set of forwards, although good in some positions, did not seem to have the overall strength, or the 'meanness' that is required to cope with the big South African forwards. Before the tour started there was speculation that perhaps the Lions might wish to play a more expansive type of game because of the obvious strength at half-back and in midfield. It was a blow therefore when Andy Irvine withdrew, not only because of his extensive capabilities, but also because of Ollie Campbell, then becoming the principal goal-kicker; the chance was lost of playing Gareth Davies at outside-half. However that problem was eventually overcome by force of circumstances. For the early part of the tour the fact remained that Irvine had been replaced by a player with about a third of his ability.

Overall I think it was a fair selection, although when I first read the names I thought it was a team that would not do tremendously well. I mentally forecast the Tests at three to South Africa and one to the Lions. However, I went out early to South Africa and saw them play against South America. That rather altered my opinion. I then thought it was possible that even this Lions team could do well, and might even win the series.

3
The African Scene

The Lions stepped off their plane at Jan Smuts Airport, Johannesburg, in warm sunshine to a warm welcome. Airport security probably kept away many people who would have liked to welcome the Lions, but there were about 1,000 waiting, although they were not allowed on the airport roofs, and had to remain in the hall and on the pavement outside.

The previous day the Springboks had won their second Test against South America, the Jaguars, by 18–9 – the first Test was won by South Africa 24–9 – and Danie Craven announced to the group of British journalists 'It was a good game; the Jaguars were good, and so were we. We'll fix you!' The grin which followed suggested that the good Doctor was not at his most serious, and no doubt his view was not shared by the majority of South African Rugby writers. They thought that the better side had lost, and that the Springboks were still some way short of finding a side good enough to beat the Lions. The Springboks had come second in everything but the two results. They had lost the scrums, the lineouts, and the rucks. Their backs had shown little idea of what to do with the ball in their hands, and had it not been for the kicking of Naas Botha, the twenty-two-year-old student at outside-half, who scored fourteen of their points with three dropped goals, a penalty goal, and a conversion, the Springboks might well have been beaten.

They had been derided prior to the match for their lack of fitness. Too many forwards carried too much weight, and that was attributed to the £30,000 sponsorship of the Dairy Control Board. It was said the Springboks were drinking an excessive amount of milk. Be that as it may, the Lions read these stories about the obesity of their opponents, listened to countless tales of how easy it would be for them to win the series, and then - decided that they would find out for themselves soon enough.

From the airport there followed a fifteen-mile bus trip to Vanderbijlpark, a small town which has grown around the steel works. Close by is Sassolburg, where oil is extracted from coal, and in case anyone should not know about the natural wealth of the area, the car registration plates bear the letters OIL. The Lions were taken away from Johannesburg to Vanderbijlpark so that they could relax during their first week in the country while the hard work of restoring tone to the bodies, which had been without a match for three or four weeks, was carried through.

Noel Murphy lost no time. Within three hours of the Lions' arrival at Vanderbijlpark he had them out training at Sassolburg. If any of the players thought it was just to be a loosener, they were gradually disillusioned. It lasted almost an hour, and by then there were some extremely tired young men, especially the heavyweights, who had to contend with the additional difficulties of training at altitude. The subdued Phil Blakeway staggered towards a crate of 'pop' groaning, 'What worries me is that it can only get worse'.

It was noticeable though that one player ran and exercised with great enthusiasm. Ollie Campbell was by now well aware that, in the absence of Irvine, he was the number one goal-kicker, and would have a very important part to play.

The next day, Monday, dawned bright and hot; an ominous sign for the players, who faced a couple of training sessions which under the glare of the sun were almost as painful to witness as to take part in. One of the busiest men during these sessions was the baggage-master Hermie Visser, who, in a period of a few minutes, was asked to cut up oranges, to blow up balls, to fill up bags of water, and to 'turn off that bloody heat lamp'. The latter request came from Fran Cotton, who was deriving little pleasure from this Indian summer.

In the morning the thirty players were cajoled into two hours of hard running, made interesting by a well-planned curriculum.

There was competitive running with the ball, quick finger-tip passing in small groups of mixed ability, the occasional game, and finally the inevitable hammering at the unit skills.

Campbell suffered a reaction from his exertions the day before, and made for the nearest physiotherapist, but reappeared in the afternoon. His combination with Terry Holmes was a fruitful exercise, as was Gareth Davies's with Colin Patterson. It was now clear that the line- and place-kicking of both Davies and Campbell would be a constant source of comparison with that of Naas Botha, the phenomenal Springbok kicker.

Serious scrummaging was reserved for the following day, and significantly it was left to Syd Millar to supervise. Millar has always considered the scrummage to be of the greatest importance. So Millar attended to the forwards and Murphy looked after the backs, while a posse of journalists watched and made notes. There were one or two who wondered whether this was the beginning of a rift in the management. Murphy was taken aback by the suggestion that the manager was interfering. 'When you have someone in the party with Syd's knowledge, surely it is good to make use of it,' he said.

Murphy certainly had plenty of experience around him to call upon. Standing track-suited on the touchline was Jack Matthews, that great Welsh centre who was a Test player for the British Lions in New Zealand in 1950, and was now the team's doctor.

Again the training was impressive. One or two of the exercises employed by the Lions on the 1971 tour to New Zealand were incorporated with the routine, whether by accident or design one did not know. The very variety of the work ensured that the players were kept interested until the end of a long session. The afternoon was devoted to set piece moves. So far there had been little time for relaxation. However, a popular form of entertainment was the fruit machine in the hotel foyer, which seemed to fox everyone but Maurice Colclough. He makes his living selling the things.

The hotel was certainly well away from the distractions of

he city. It was out in the country with a river on which there were boats, swimming pools, a golf course, tennis courts, a gymnasium and a health hydro.

That Monday evening there was an excellent barbecue which did much to make the players forget their aches and pains. The journalists were glad to notice that the players mixed readily with the Press. Perhaps they had to do so; the Press outnumbered the players by two to one.

Maybe things were going too well. The Wednesday training session was taken with the same hard grafting, and was followed by even fiercer scrummaging, with packs going at each other like stags in the mating season. It was not long before the Gloucester tight-head prop Phil Blakeway had his opposite number Fran Cotton on his knees. Cotton, of course, eventually worked things out, but it was clear that Test places were to be fought hard for by everyone.

At the end of the session the team for the opening match against Eastern Province was announced, and Cotton was one of the six 1977 Lions in the pack. Peter Wheeler and Graham Price made up the remainder of the front row. Bill Beaumont and Allan Martin were paired in the second row, and the back row had a possible Test look to it with Stuart Lane and Jeff Squire on the flanks and the immensely promising John Beattie at number eight. As we had expected the Irish and Welsh half-backs were split, with Holmes partnering Campbell, who went off that afternoon to practise his kicking with the former Springbok outside-half Gerald Bosch.

The wings were Elgan Rees and Mike Slemen, the centres David Richards and Gravell, and Bruce Hay was at fullback. Later in the day Millar broke the news that Richards's father had died and that Dai would be returning home that night. The news was not entirely unexpected. Mr Richards had been suffering from cancer for some time, but it was his dearest wish that his son should go to South Africa with the Lions and represent them on the field. So Richards departed and decided to rejoin the party the following week.

With him on the plane to London was Ken Rowlands, the

Welsh referee who had been in charge of the two Tests that the Springboks had played against the Jaguars. Rowlands had met Millar the previous day to discuss the problems that the Lions might face from South African referees. Millar knew from bitter experience that these problems were many and varied. This time, however, at long last the principle of neutral referees for the Tests had been accepted. Of all the countries on the International Board, New Zealand had been the most reluctant over this, but even they will eventually agree. So two Frenchmen, Jean-Pierre Bonnet and Francis Palmade, had been appointed to share the Test series. In one way it might make the provincial matches more difficult for the Tourists, for without the incentive of a Test match to come local referees had little to lose, and might be giving some eccentric decisions.

The Lions had their seventh training session in five days and began to show signs of wear. The session on the Thursday morning was an untidy affair with the Saturday side making heavy weather of their work. Perhaps too much was being asked of the players. They had worked willingly and deserved a break. In any event it proved too much for Campbell, who had still not fully recovered from his exertions on the Sunday, and was moving with less freedom than he had shown on that occasion. Because of his importance to the team it was thought imprudent to risk him, and Gareth Davies was brought in to partner Holmes at half-back.

The final session before the first match was certainly more impressive. The back line moved smoothly outside Davies, more smoothly in fact than it had done with Campbell, who is fractionally more laboured in his passing. By now the players were interested only in getting on with the matches. Their initiation was unlikely to be gentle.

The match against Eastern Province had in the past always proved to be hard. It was during this encounter in 1974 that the infamous '99 call' was instigated. This was a distress signal readily answered by the rest of the Lions, and was an awesome distortion of that gallant principle, all for one and one for all. Unfortunately in the Provincial side there lurked a centre by the name of Dennis Campher, who had not been entirely blameless six years previously. His reputation had not improved in the intervening years. There would be no need however this time to call '99', although by the end of the match the Lions were to lose their fastest loose forward and have their outside-half sidelined for at least three weeks.

Springboks in Disarray

by Carwyn James

Following the Springboks' winning, but sub-standard, performances against the lively Jaguars, 'Butch' Lochner, the convenor of the Springboks' selectors, decided to plan two training camps for a squad of twenty-four players before announcing their team to play the Lions in the first Test. Danie Craven, who is a South African representative on the International Board, would not hear of it. According to him the plan contravened the International Board ruling.

I would have thought that the period of time spent at the training camp was probably the relevant issue, because in the United Kingdom each country holds squad sessions on a Sunday and a Thursday before international matches. For home matches the players are back at work on the Monday and on the Friday. Such a squad session could have been held easily in Johannesburg or Pretoria, particularly as most of the squad lived in and played for Transvaal or Northern Transvaal. The other players came from Western Province. The problem was that in the Transvaal healthy exercise is frowned upon on Sunday, on religious or puritanical grounds. Dr Craven saw no exception to holding further trials, an easy extension of the training camp problem, which will not raise an eyebrow in Wales or in Wellington.

It is amazing that Lochner and Craven had not discussed this simple problem before, and that in 1980 the left hand of South Africa did not know what the right hand was doing. But of course there had been little international competition in South Africa for so long that the International Board was a distant, almost non-existent, body for all but the Doctor.

What amazed me was that this minor problem made headline news while another contravention, a far more serious one, went unheeded. Nellie Smith, the National Director of Coaching, a professional man, was allowed to coach the national amateur team. This concept is frowned upon by all the other members of the International Board including France. Italy, in the person of Pierre Villepreux, naturally is an exception. At provincial level as well, directors of coaching in South Africa were allowed to coach the provincial team. How was it possible within the framework of an amateur game for a professional man to coach and select an amateur team? Dr Craven defended the principle, but had to give in to the International Board ruling, the contravention of which had not, as I thought, gone unheeded. The South African Rugby Board announced during the tour that they were happy to abide by the International Board's ruling, and accordingly Nellie Smith and Ian Kirkpatrick, a national selector, would not be able to choose Springbok teams in future seasons. They would have to give up those duties at the end of the current South African season.

4
Early
Drama

The sky was again clear and the ground bathed in sparkling sunshine when the Lions caught the afternoon plane from Johannesburg two days before their first match in Port Elizabeth. Now the excitement grew; the tour was really on. We tried to imagine how the Lions would be received when they took the field in the Boet Erasmus Stadium, named after a local worthy who is still alive and well in his eightieth year living in Port Elizabeth. He is a Rugby fanatic, has watched Test matches since 1928, and saw the first Test ever played at the ground between South Africa and Scotland in 1960.

The ground can hold 55,000 people, and it still bears some of the legacies of the bad old days. To the right of the main stand is a grass mound with wooden crush barriers. It was there that the black people had to go in the old days, and there they could see little, for usually they had to face a blinding sun.

Now it is different. The crowd is fully integrated. Black people can buy a ticket and go to any part of the ground they wish, that is if they can afford it. No doubt some still go to the grass mound, which used to be called Kaffir Corner, just because they meet their friends there.

Although the ground was not full there was a good crowd when the Lions came out and were given a tumultuous welcome. One would have liked to see more black people in the crowd but there was no doubt of the warmth of the welcome. At last it was happening; the Lions were playing in South Africa again. The pitch which they ran on to, jumping and stretching their arms and legs, is one of the finest in the country. The covering is blue Kentucky grass beautifully prepared by the groundsmen.

Before the match was a minute old, Stuart Lane, coming off the back of the first lineout, stumbled as he went to tackle the Province outside-half, Gavin Cowley, and appeared to turn his ankle. Lane knew exactly what he had done, and before Bill Beaumont had come over to enquire about his health, the Welshman was signalling to those on the touchline for assistance. He had damaged the lateral ligament in his right knee. For Lane it was the end of the tour.

Lane himself was not at all certain about the future of his Rugby career. It was not the first time he had had the injury. He was assured of a place in the record books, though. No Lion has had a shorter playing record, with the possible exception of Nial Brophy, who broke a leg in the first minute of the first match of the Lions tour to Australia and New Zealand in 1959. That could be little consolation to Lane, or the Lions, who were left without a specialist open-side flanker. Lane was replaced in the match by Derek Quinnell, who in training had shown even less enthusiasm than usual, but Quinnell in a match is a different man altogether. He and Jeff Squire were the outstanding players of the game.

Still, the fact remained that the Lions' back row was ponderous, and if the Eastern Province outside-half Cowley had spotted that, then he might have made life very difficult for the Lions. Not that it was ever easy. At no time were the Lions able to dominate any phase of the play. They were not helped either by inconsistent refereeing, a constant hazard with which touring sides must quickly come to terms.

It was also apparent that the Lions would have to solve the problem of the bouncing ball. In this respect it was difficult not to feel some sympathy for Bruce Hay, who had a most unhappy afternoon at fullback. Too often he was caught out of position, and his sluggishness over the ground hardly bore the mark of an international wing. Perhaps if Gareth Davies had remained on the field he would not have been so horribly exposed. Davies had been playing beautifully, and in spite of missing a penalty from in front of the posts, he had been successful with two, had dropped a goal, and had made a break from which Mike Slemen had scored the opening try of the tour. As Slemen was taking the awkward pass off his toes, Davies was landing on the point of his shoulder with sufficient force to cause a dislocation.

The immediate numbness in the area enabled him to take the conversion without too much discomfort, but then feeling returned and the change in the general outline of his shoulder was enough for him to seek medical opinion.

It was hardly surprising that the Lions, having already lost Lane, and being as yet unaccustomed to each other, also lost such rhythm as was beginning to show. Peter Morgan moved in from the centre to outside-half and Jim Renwick came on in the centre. Eastern Province also required both their replacements, and with so many comings and goings the game failed to produce sustained quality. The Province, with a try by Chris Heunis, closed to within five points of the Lions and pressed hard. Just before half-time the Lions scored a second try. They managed to get a good shove going in the scrum and Holmes drove over to touch down, Renwick converting.

The crisis seemed to be over, and at half-time the Lions held a comfortable if somewhat flattering lead of 21–10. They went further ahead soon afterwards when Elgan Rees raced in at the corner after some superb build-up work by the back row – Squire, Quinnell and Beattie. It was too far out for Renwick to convert, and almost immediately the Province responded when Hay failed to gather a long kick in front of his posts. From the resulting scrum Dennis Campher took a short pass from his outside-half and went over between the posts. The try was converted and again the Lions were under pressure. A forty-metre penalty goal by Renwick brought the relief they needed, and towards the end they were beginning to work out a few of their problems, particularly in the scrum, where the Province forwards had coped admirably, and had slewed the Lions to such an extent that much of the Lions' possession was rendered useless.

With a little more experience Beattie might have been better able to cope with this, but he showed enough promise to suggest that he would be making a very strong bid for a Test place. His play drew praise from his rival for that place, Quinnell, who said that by the end of the tour Beattie would be an exceptionally fine player, although he had still got a lot to learn.

That applied equally to the Lions as a whole, a fact which Murphy afterwards acknowledged, although he praised their courage in difficult circumstances.

Bill Beaumont seemed fairly happy with the 28–16 victory. He said it was better to win by twelve points at that stage than by thirty; then there would be no complacency.

That evening when it was discovered that a Northern Transvaal kicking machine named Botha had contributed nineteen of his side's points in their 31–12 Currie Cup win over Transvaal, there was even less reason for complacency.

Carwyn James sums it all up like this:

The Lions lacked control. That was evident in their scrummaging, particularly on their own put-in when they allowed their opponents to use the wheel as a disruptive ploy. That was a feature of the game in the United Kingdom during the whole of the season, and the scrummage became almost as untidy as the lineout. To counter the wheel the left, or the loose-head side, must give a little while the right or the tight-head side drives really hard to balance the clockwise movement of the disruptive shove. Another precautionary measure is to crab sideways to the right. A touring team should be capable of these sophistications. At the lineout there were too many gaps in the Lions' formation, and this must have given Holmes nightmares. The same malaise was apparent in the fourth match of the 1974 tour, also against Eastern Province, when Gareth Edwards was at the receiving end. On the Monday after the game Syd Millar in a quiet but adamant tone of voice told his troops, 'I'm telling you that is not going to happen ever again on this tour'. What Millar said, went. The Springboks, when they played against South America, did their best to control and then drive from the lineouts. Well versed in the tactic, forwards like Silva soon put a stop to their drive, and that left them barren of ideas.

Occasionally the Lions drove the ball well from the lineout, but they had yet to master the technique of rolling the ball when they were stopped. This is a matter of much practice and calls for precise control at the crucial moment. It should have been the goal of the Lions to have perfected this technique before the first Test. Murphy and Millar worked hard with them in the first week, but one knows it is almost impossible to cover all aspects of play thoroughly before going into the first match. I was delighted to see the ball being bounced from one player to another so that they could get the feel of the ground, the turf, and the ball at the Boet Erasmus Stadium the day before the match.

I had an uneasy feeling though that they did not practise enough of the Garyowen, the kigh kick into the sun, to see if the players could get used to the glare, and to measuring distances in conditions so different from those at home where it is easy to assess speed and distances in the mellow light. It must take golfers and cricketers who go from Europe to South Africa a long time to acclimatize.

It was strange to see Slemen, a man of immense footballing ability, turning and missing a high ball by more than a metre. Hay had a most forgettable day, and his lack of fitness could not have helped his judgement. On days like that the Lions would have been well advised to take the field at least fifteen minutes before the kick-off.

The loss of Lane within fifty seconds meant that they had to play a much closer game forward. There was no quick man to get to the point of breakdown. It also meant that there was little assistance for the midfield defence, a fact which Cowley noticed too late in the game. The alignment of the Lions' back defence was faulty; one centre getting ahead of his outside-half and co-centre can open up huge gaps for an alert attack. Gravell was so incensed with the play of Campher that he kept looking for a chance to make his physical presence felt. This kind of thing can give personal pleasure but much pain to the team. Gravell's contribution in fact was enormous, but it lacked control so necessary at this level.

Before Davies left the field the line moved reasonably smoothly and with some rhythm, but as soon as he had gone the machine lost all its lubrication, and everything was done hurriedly and in fits and starts.

As an elder statesman and as the captain-elect of Llanelli for the following season, Gravell wanted to protect his young protégé Peter Morgan. Morgan loves running with the ball, and hates kicking it. No doubt he had visions too of his nightmare experience against Ireland at Lansdowne Road when his clearance kick was charged down and Ireland scored a try. So Gravell took over, and in doing so he naturally assumed the mantle of Ian MacRae or Joggie Jansen as he has so often done for Wales. This crash-ball bullocking down the middle of the field is the kind of game which plays into the hands of the likes of the hard-tackling Campher, who is a back-row forward by instinct playing in the centre. The Lions I thought will not win matches by crash-balling down the middle. The Eastern Province gamble under the guidance of their general, Cowley, of throwing long passes in their threequarter attacks paid off. Whenever they moved the ball they looked dangerous, more dangerous than the Lions.

They failed, however, to find the Lions' most vulnerable point in defence. Campher earned for himself again the title of 'Dennis the Menace'. His high tackle on Slemen could have decapitated his victim. His very late tackle too on the unbalanced Rees, who had tried to drop a goal, was vicious. When Cowley took Davies's legs, Campher did the rest, and Davies looked likely to be out for at least three weeks. In one game alone Campher won enough yellow cards to keep him out for the rest of the season. Compared with Campher, Paul Ringer, who was suffering what was virtually a life sentence for a dubious late tackle, was an angel. I thought then, 'If there are any more Camphers around, and weak referees and touch-judges, there will be a steady flow of player replacements between the United Kingdom and South Africa.'

5
Lane Replaced

Sunday, the day after the first match, brought the news that a replacement would be required for Stuart Lane, and that Gareth Davies, who had strained a joint at the end of his collar-bone, would be out of action for about three weeks, but would be staying on the tour. Naturally there was immediate speculation about Lane's replacement. Fergus Slattery and Tony Neary had said they would be available only for the last six weeks of the tour, and there was no reason to suppose that either would change his mind. On the other hand there was no harm in trying, and the situation was desperate enough. However, neither could be persuaded, and in fact much later in the tour Neary was asked again, and was still not available.

Another possibility to replace Lane was the Scot, David Leslie, who had withdrawn from Scotland's tour of France with a shoulder injury. There was also the uncapped Bridgend forward Gareth Williams, who was in North America with Wales. Both men had the right qualifications; they are fast over the ground, and tall enough to act as auxiliary jumpers at the tail of the lineout. Leslie was the first choice, and was approached by Mickey Steele-Bodger during the weekend. The shoulder injury which prevented him from going to France was still troubling him, and his answer was conditional upon passing a medical examination. That he failed. Williams had had a fine season, though reserving his best for the Welsh Cup Final against Swansea, when he was easily the outstanding player on the field. He had one enormous advantage too. His presence with the Wales party in America meant that he was fit, and would need little time to acclimatize to South African conditions. So Williams was chosen, but by the time he arrived it was almost a week since Lane had been injured.

On this tour the Lions broke with the tradition of Sunday travel. With one or two exceptions they had decided to set aside Sunday as a day of rest, and travel to the next destination on Monday. It made a good deal of sense, and the players welcomed it, but it also cut their social activities to some extent.

The Monday journey from Port Elizabeth to East London, where the next match was against the South African Rugby Association Invitation XV, was short enough to tempt half of the Fleet Street journalists to go by road and enjoy the superb coastal scenery. Unfortunately one group had made such a horrible mess of converting kilometres into miles per hour that they roared into a speed trap at something approaching terminal velocity. It so happened that the custodian of the law into whose trap the luckless trio had fallen was apparently just about the only person in South Africa who knew nothing about the Lions tour, and was therefore totally impervious to bribes of badges, Test tickets, or anything else. The situation was very grave. The speedsters were informed that they were within five miles an hour of a prison sentence, and that they could expect a fine of at least 200 rands (about £90). There was nothing for it but some moist-eyed humility, which, after about half an hour, began to take effect. Eventually three of Britain's most distinguished Rugby writers were sent on their way with nothing more than a stern warning.

Meanwhile the Lions were going through their own kind of hell. Noel Murphy had not been overjoyed by their opening display against Eastern Province and was making the players work harder than ever. At the end of the work the forwards and backs split up, the forwards to scrummage and work on a counter to the wheel. Eventually they appeared to be content that there would be no repetition of the previous Saturday's embarrassment. Meanwhile the backs worked on their alignment, which had been so ragged.

Their next opponents, the South African Rugby Association, is one of the ruling bodies for black players, the other being the

South African Rugby Union, which claimed to be responsible for more than 90 per cent of all black players in the country. SARA, and just about everyone else, disputed these figures, which certainly appeared to be highly exaggerated. SARA is affiliated to the South African Rugby Board; SARU refused to have anything to do with either.

In 1974 the Lions had played a match against SARA, or the Leopards as they were known, and although the Tourists won by 56–10, the Leopards had put up a very creditable performance. Such was the state of their Rugby in 1980, though, that they were forced to invite eight white players to bolster up their side. Already they had lost to a Northern Transvaal Under-25 team by eighty points, and by fifty points to South West Africa, who are in the third division of Provincial Rugby. The announcement that the Leopards were to include white players surprised Syd Millar, who had received no prior warning of it. Still he had no complaints; in fact he welcomed it because it increased the number of matches that the Lions would be playing against multi-racial sides.

Among the white players were Ewoud Malan, who had toured Britain with the Barbarians, and Thys Burger, a back-row forward from Northern Transvaal who was on the fringe of Springbok selection. For this game he would be playing at No. 8, the position that the South African captain holds in the Springbok side, so Burger's best bet appeared to be on the flank. This was the first time that the Lions had played against a multi-racial side in South Africa.

The Lions' selection gave a chance to those who had not played the previous Saturday, with the exception of Ollie Campbell who was still feeling the effects of his hamstring strain. He trained gently by himself. He looked a long way from being fit, although Millar assured everyone that Campbell would be fit to play against Natal on the following Saturday. With David Richards rejoining the party that day it was felt that the Lions were well covered at outside-half, and bearing in mind Campbell's importance, it would be unwise to risk him at that time.

In the afternoon following Murphy's training session one or

two players had just enough energy left to go on the golf course. The course, called Eastbank, is reckoned by no less a judge than Gary Player to be one of the finest in South Africa. Whether he would care to say the same of it after the Lions had finished playing must be open to question. Four months without rain had left the ground so hard and the fairways so threadbare that it was necessary to tee up the ball before every shot. Such was the standard of the Lions' golf that anything smaller than a football sitting on the tee-pegs had little chance of being hit. The only player who came anywhere near to being 'under par' was Fran Cotton, and when he bent to pick his ball out of a hole he found it perching on top of a python. His scheming team-mates had not told him that the python was very dead, and that they had put it there.

A postscript which emerged from the replacement tale, and the inevitable investigation which was made, revealed that the initial approach to David Leslie about his availability should he be required as a replacement, was made only the week before the Lions left. That seemed uncommonly short notice to give to a man who might have to spend two months or more away from family and business. With all the interest in the replacement for Lane, the match against SARA was almost of secondary importance.

The match might have been affected too by the publication the day before of the British Sports Council's report on their mission to South Africa, but it was not. Much to the delight of the SARA officials the match day was a great success. There was no evidence of a boycott, and there were few empty spaces among the crowd of 10,000.

On the basis that it was wrong to make any enduring judgement after the Lions' opening match, so it would have been unwise to be too harsh on the Wednesday side. There were fewer excuses to be made, though. The Tourists had had four more days in which to become acclimatized, and more important, the SARA XV, strengthened as it was by the eight white players, was far more of a scratch combination than the Lions. Many of the failings which had come to light against Eastern Province were again apparent. At least the scrummage looked more secure, although in the matter of tight heads the game ended with two apiece.

The Lions began well enough with a penalty goal from the touch-line, kicked by Clive Woodward. Considering that Woodward was fourth in line as a kicker of goals in his club, Leicester, one felt it was a demonstration of how badly off the Lions were for experts in this crucial area. On the day Woodward did extremely well, though. He succeeded with everything he kicked, collecting sixteen points with three penalties, a dropped goal, and two conversions.

Jim Renwick, who shared the kicking duties, failed with three attempts. In spite of their superior scrummaging the Lions looked vulnerable in defence, and around the fringes of the scrum, where neither Colm Tucker nor John O'Driscoll looked happy. On several occasions they were left stranded by the little black scrum-half, William Speelman.

Mercifully Rodney O'Donnell proved to be far steadier at full-back than Hay had been against Eastern Province, but his line kicking was hardly up to the standard of his fielding. One shuddered to think what someone of Naas Botha's ability as a dropped goal kicker would have made of such carelessness. The Lions' half-time lead of 13–3 reflected badly upon them. The only try of the half had been scored by Derek Quinnell after a typically barging run from the back of the scrum. Quinnell, captain for the day, was finding it hard to cope with Burger at the back of the lineout. Burger did a good job in front of the Springbok selectors. He had a lot to thank his friends for in the lineout. Time and again they propelled him skywards under the nose of a most lenient referee. Some of the referee's decisions caused such bewilderment among the Lions that Quinnell had to devote much of his time to earnest discussion with him. It was doubtful if the Welshman was any the wiser at the end of it all.

SARA were the first to score in the second half when their outside-half Ferdie Prinsloo kicked a second penalty goal for a late tackle. In the final quarter, the Invitation XV having had much of the sap drawn from them, the Lions scored fifteen points to give them a winning margin they scarcely deserved. First Woodward dropped a neat goal after some good running by John Carleton. Then came one of the better moments of the match. Colin Patterson, who had played erratically at the base of the scrum, ran to the open side and kicked into the box on the blind side for Elgan Rees, haring up on the left, to gather on the bounce and run over for a try between the posts, giving Woodward a simple conversion. It was reminiscent of the move made by Gareth Edwards and J.J. Williams on the Lions tour six years before.

The final try was again by Quinnell, and again it came from a drive from the scrummage. As if the management had not enough to occupy their minds, Phil Blakeway, who had become slower and slower as the game progressed, came off near the end holding his ribs. He had aggravated an injury which had been troubling him all season, and had caused him to have pain killers before two internationals. That evening he seemed in little discomfort, and the next day he was able to train, but when the party arrived in Durban he went to hospital for a precautionary X-ray.

Woe and Worry

by Carwyn James

Wednesday's child was full of woe and worry. Apart from the last ten minutes when they scored fifteen points, the Lions looked pathetically unco-ordinated and lacked poise. It was as if they had given in to the nagging thoughts that the environment was so different, that they were wearing Lions' jerseys which had never before played a multi-racial team, and that the opposition was bound to be of the highest class. Morgan Cuchse's team was nothing of the kind. It was a scratch combination which contained some good players but more less good players.

Solomon Mhlaba at full-back played better than the Springbok Pierre Edwards had done against the South Americans. Timothy Nkonki looked a lively customer on the wing. The huge Transvaaler, Franz Weltz, was both creative and a nuisance; Cuchse himself did the work of two, and Burger might have earned himself a Test place on the flank instead of Stofberg if he could repeat his performance the following week.

Perhaps the referee Jimmy Smith-Belton bothered the Lions. Ten penalties shared in the first twenty minutes ensured that the referee was seen, heard, and observed centre stage for a full eighty-minute star performance. Initially Quinnell was the Lloyd-George type of diplomat, but the interpretation of the lineout laws and the number of people in the lineout so puzzled him that eventually he just shrugged his shoulders in bewilderment and silence.

In discomfort, despite the illegal pain-relieving injections prior to the match, Blakeway tried to protect his ribs by packing at such an angle that the opposing hooker became a menace to Alan Phillips. This angular packing can lead to the occasional winning of a tight-head, but in this game four were shared and so no material advantage was gained. Occasionally the Lions walked the opposition into retreat on their ball, but too often on their own ball they fell for the sudden wheel. Countering the wheel must have been still high on Murphy's programme.

The Irish flankers enjoyed a busy afternoon. Neither O'Driscoll nor Tucker will ever achieve greatness, but both will always give value for those who believe that workrate is a high priority. Alan Tomes and Maurice Colclough were disappointing in the lineout and in general play. Neither was anywhere near international standard. Both were already doomed to be Saturday dirt-truckers unless they could pull themselves together quickly and realize that this was a country that breeds hard men to play in the engine room.

Colin Patterson is an exciting little player who is capable of getting the ball away at speed, particularly off the ground. Even in this match he showed touches of class. His chip into the box for instance gave Elgan Rees his second try of the tour, but too often Patterson was too fussy. He oscillated around like a scalded cat and sometimes David Richards went one way and he another. On this form Terry Holmes was in another frame.

Richards, playing his first game, and probably travel-weary, was prominent as a beautifully balanced runner, but he never seemed to be the general at peace with himself and the world. The threequarter line hardly moved smoothly. Renwick was inconsistent, and only Woodward looked a player of class. Carleton was ponderous and unsure.

At full-back Rodney O'Donnell played well enough, but with little imagination yet for the counter-attack. A man of super-stition, he must have suffered agonies when the Lions were stuck on the figure thirteen for the best part of forty-five minutes. O'Donnell's superstitions were a minor sensation in South Africa. He refuses to walk on lines, and so must zig-zag across hotel foyers. He must be last on the bus, and last into the changing room. He cannot go on to the field three times. When Ireland played France he had to go on the field for inspection, and then the French asked him to go on for a photograph. This was a terrible problem and O'Donnell refused until Noel Murphy undertook full responsibility for whatever happened to him in the game that day. He has great trouble going to bed because he must not touch the bottom sheet or the top sheet with one part of his body. He throws off the cover and jumps into bed, landing on his back so that all his body touches the bed. At home he has to walk out of his door backwards. He has so many superstitions that he cannot always remember them all.

So, to sum up, the Lions started this match well and finished it well, but the middle bit was a bore. The occasional rolling ball, and the solid scrummaging were bonus points, but the disappointment was the casual lack of urgency of the players, who failed to motivate themselves. The series unquestionably would be won by players hungry for success, and at that moment the Lions lacked the winning, let alone the killer instinct.

6
Shades of
Izak van Heerden
by Carwyn James

'You are a non-conformist and a bloody dictator.' Such was Dr Danie Craven's assessment of Roger Gardner, the present director of coaching, and the coach of Natal, the province which the Lions were to play at King's Park, Durban. The words apply equally well to the good Doctor himself, and possibly to any coach of standing who takes his work seriously. The domination of coaches by less professionally minded selectors is a curse to the modern game. The job of selector, too, is a serious one which every committee man in the land thinks he can do. Not all of them can.

Gardner's career embraces Caerphilly Grammar School, a year with John Robins, a former Lions coach, at Loughborough Colleges, three years with Martin Underwood, the former England international, at St Luke's College, three years with Danie Craven at Newlands in Western Province, South Africa, and now, in the wake of Izak van Heerden, he coaches Natal. Along the way he came under the spell of Ray Williams, Coaching Organizer for Wales, and qualified on his coaching courses. Gardner took his expertise to Cape Town, and for two years taught at Bishops Diocesan School where Canon George Ogilvie first launched Rugby Football in South Africa. The game is still a way of life at the sporting school, where Basil Bey, according to Gardner, is a superb coach, and an inspiration to both the masters and the pupils.

As director of coaching at Newlands, Gardner found the next three years were equally stimulating. Newlands is the home of the South African Rugby Board, and the second home of Danie Craven, who has been President of the Board for twenty-five years. His other home is at Stellenbosch University, where he is director of sport. Scores of pilgrims, myself included, have made the trek to see Danie's mechanical inventions to aid the techniques of scrummaging, lineouts, mauling, rucking, and driving. In his books on the game – for years he has been a prolific writer – he always includes photographs of his complex circuits, more befitting a course for hardening commandos than maturing Rugby players. Craven is proud of the Stellenbosch way, an accepted tough close pattern of play based on solid scrummaging and the fundamentals of the forward game. A former Springbok scrum-half famous for his dive-pass, Craven has a keen awareness of the value of tight forward play, the key to winning Rugby. For more than half a century he has been the voice of South African Rugby, and the world has usually listened. He was still at it even in his seventieth year.

The previous season, following two defeats, the Western Province captain, Morne du Plessis, was at his wits' end and on the point of resigning after about ninety appearances as captain of his Province. Dr Craven summoned him and announced that for the rest of the season he would take on the role of adviser to the official coach, Appies du Toit. He also announced that the side would not lose another game. The Stellenbosch pattern was adopted. Ten of his University students were in the squad, and over cups of tea daily the Doctor of Psychology applied his theories on that subject allied to the game he loves.

As Morne du Plessis said, 'Doc is a remarkable person. He never talks about the possibility of losing a match.' Craven's prediction came true. They did not lose another match, and they shared the Currie Cup with a strong Northern Transvaal side. 'They would never have done it without Doc,' was Roger Gardner's testimony. By that time Gardner had left Western Province, and ironically it was his new Province, Natal, that had inflicted one of the two defeats which inspired Craven's intervention.

In the museum at King's Park, Durban, hangs a photograph of the late Izak van Heerden, a perceptive thinker of the game, a philosopher, a man ahead of his time. A fortnight before this match, while watching the Pumas, dressed as Jaguars, I felt the presence of a crowd of witnesses, foremost among them being van Heerden, who was a major influence on the development of the game in the Argentine. He was a major influence on the game in Natal too, as former players like Keith Oxlee and Tommy Bedford would readily testify. I always found van Heerden's ideas more easily digestible than those of the Doctor. Van Heerden accepted Doc's cold, calculating, classical concepts, but added to them a more expansive dimension which allowed for flair and imagination.

In the wrong hands, of course, this dimension could be spoiled with looseness, and it was just that which Gardner had inherited just over a year previously in Natal.

At Port Elizabeth the previous weekend Gardner had been doing his spying bit. He was conversant with the strengths and weaknesses of Eastern Province, and was therefore in a better position than most of us to evaluate the performance of the Lions.

It was a sub-standard performance which was repeated by the other team on the Wednesday; full of the stresses and strains of young men wearing Lions' jerseys for the first time, many of them overawed by the new environment, and over-estimating their opponents. Gardner, the exiled Welshman, saw weaknesses too, and pointed to one by enquiring why Gordon Brown, the best lock in the world, was not in the party. He was critical of the Springbok policy of playing left and right flankers instead of playing Rob Louw, a quick man like Lane, Neary, or Ringer, on the open side. I wondered how much of the British free-playing style reminiscent of Izak van Heerden, the traditional game of Natal, and how much of Dr Craven's Stellenbosch game would be evident. When I put the question to Gardner he just smiled, but I would not have been surprised to see a little bit of Welsh cunning of the Llanbradach kind, and with Mark Loane, the former Wallaby captain, normally a No. 8 but down to play on the flank in this game, possibly a little Australian cunning as well.

By then, with the first test at Newlands only a fortnight and four matches away, it was inevitable that we should be thinking of the Lions Test team. It was important of course to have a strong side out against Natal, and perhaps it should have been necessary to experiment a little. For that reason I would have had Peter Morgan at full-back, and Clive Woodward on the right wing because he has a natural outward swerve to the right, and neither of the right wings had shown by then that they were Test material. I would also have had John O'Driscoll as open-side flanker.

In fact the selectors chose O'Donnell at full-back, which meant that they were opting for safety rather than providing an extra dimension in attack. They did not put Woodward on the wing at this stage. That was to come later. For this game they chose John Carleton. Colm Tucker was in the back row, not O'Driscoll; otherwise their choice coincided with mine. Gravell, Richards and Slemen were the other threequarters. Ollie Campbell was chosen to make his first appearance of the tour, and to play in partnership with Terry Holmes for the first time. He was also given the leadership of the backs. The front five were Cotton, Wheeler, Price, Martin and Beaumont; John Beattie was at No. 8, flanked by Tucker and Squire.

Apparently John Beattie felt a bit depressed after watching Derek Quinnell's display on the Wednesday. He thought Quinnell had played himself into the Saturday side. Obviously the selection committee did not share that view.

The lineout command enjoyed by Thys Burger at the tail was further evidence that Quinnell was not equipped to compete in that department, and as the Springboks were likely to depend upon Morne du Plessis for much of their lineout possession the Lions would want to have a counter. On the other hand, though, by picking Beattie the Lions were denied the experience of Quinnell, whose physical and mental hardness would be such an asset in a match of this importance. It would be an important day in the young life of John Beattie.

It was an important day for Campbell too, as the No. 1 goal-kicker and back line general, and he was not likely to be allowed much room for manoeuvre by Natal's back row, which, besides

Loane, included their captain Wynand Claassen, a Springbok trials No. 8.

The Lions trained at East London and before leaving for Durban announced their side, which contained a dozen, maybe thirteen, of the Test XV.

7
Victory in Injury Time

The Lions' match-plan against Natal at King's Park, Durban, was to subdue the opposition by playing controlled Rugby and then to run them into the ground. As it turned out the subjugation lasted less than twenty minutes, and after that it was Natal who ran the Lions into the ground. In the end the Tourists were fortunate to scrape through with a 21–15 victory.

There were mitigating circumstances. The enervating atmosphere inside the Stadium, where the temperature went well up into the 80s, turned the Lions' jerseys a deeper shade of scarlet within minutes of the kick-off. Eventually the Lions showed great character, scoring the winning try in injury time, but it was evident that much needed doing to the team with little time to do it before the Test.

The Lions began promisingly enough playing to their plan. No attempts were made to run the ball. Ollie Campbell concentrated on kicking for position, which was much appreciated by the forwards, who even at that stage were feeling the pace. The first back line move, when it came, ended with the Lions scoring from a most unlikely source. The ball went astray midfield, and was salvaged by the ever alert Mike Slemen, who dropped a goal.

Soon afterwards the Lions were awarded a penalty close enough for Campbell to be called up. The South Africans had waited patiently for this moment, which almost inevitably turned out to be an anti-climax. As the ball veered wildly towards the corner flag, the Republic, almost to a man, heaved a mighty sigh of relief. No doubt they thought this man Campbell was no Naas Botha. It was clear though that Campbell, playing his first game for six weeks, was not fully fit. Later he kicked two penalty goals and a conversion, but he was naturally reluctant to overstretch himself. In fact he was responsible for setting up the winning try, and the Lions had much to thank him for.

They led 6–3 at half-time with Slemen's dropped goal and one of Campbell's penalties against a penalty goal by Natal's Cliffie Brown, a wing of startling pace. Campbell and Brown swopped penalty goals early in the second half, but Natal, showing more confidence in themselves, displayed a great deal more initiative in attack than the Lions. Their back row was outstanding, Wally Watt a very promising young player, in particular showing up in the most unlikely situations, helped considerably, it is true, by the referee's strange interpretation of the off-side law.

In the scrum Graham Price came under unexpected pressure from a young bull of a man called Mort Mortassagne, who was talked of as the new Piet du Toit. None of the writers present could remember seeing Price in such difficulties. The Lions held an advantage of sorts in the lineout where Allan Martin took some fine two-handed catches, but too often Terry Holmes had to deal with badly directed tap-backs. This he did magnificently, and if occasionally he was caught in possession, it was no fault of his.

Holmes, in fact, did the donkey work for his own try. He kicked into the box from a scrum, but Slemen over-ran the ball a metre from the Natal line. From the resulting scrum the Lions went for the pushover, were held up, and left it for Holmes to force his way over. Any feeling that Natal were finished vanished when Tim Cox, a most adventurous full-back, began a sweeping movement inside his own twenty-two which ended in Mortassagne arising last from a pile of players on the Lions line, the ball in his hand, and a look of undisguised delight on his face. Brown converted.

Had the score remained level at 15–15 the Lions could hardly have complained, but in injury time the hitherto subdued Campbell set off on a jinking run which took him to within fifteen metres of the Natal line. The ball came back to Holmes, who again chose the right option, feeding Ray Gravell on the short side. Outside Gravell was John Carleton, who seconds before had been led limping to the touchline. The try-line was undefended, and Carleton took Gravell's perfect pass to score the winning try between the posts, which Slemen converted.

Again Murphy had cause to praise the Lions' courage, but courage alone would not win Test matches. John Beattie had probably played himself out of the Test side, albeit temporarily. There were times when he seemed uncertain as to where to go next on the field, and although he ran himself into the ground, his running seldom bore fruit. There was no disgrace in that. He remained the most promising Scottish forward since Gordon Brown, and Scotland would derive great benefit from the lessons that Beattie learned on this tour.

These are Carwyn James's thoughts on the match:

Syd Millar made the comment that Lions teams in South Africa never play as well on the coast as they do on the Veldt. Both he and Noel Murphy were rather disappointed that their team, including as it did a dozen of the probable Test side, had not made sure of victory in the first quarter. During that time they showed more determination and venom than they had before, but they lost control and that almost cost them the game.

The British Press and the management were bitterly critical of the loose refereeing at the lineouts, and in all phases of play relating to the off-side law. As a result the backs suffered a great deal, but I thought at the time that they should have read the situation better and aligned more deeply. Their counter was to kick away possession, which only created other pressure situations from a running full-back like Cox, and fast wings like Brown and Lauri Sharp.

In hot humid summer-like conditions which favoured the home side scrummaging must have been a painful test of strength and stamina. The Lions coped. They coped less well at the lineouts, which was still the problem child. Bill Beaumont hardly took a clean ball. Martin took some two-handed catches in style, and Jeff Squire, well as he played, suffered from an early bump. Beattie looked inexperienced, but Colm Tucker played the vigorous Munster game like a good man of Shannon. Already the Test team was taking shape, with Cotton, Wheeler, Price, Martin and Beaumont as the front five. It was clear the back row must include Squire and Quinnell, and Tucker should be played if Gareth Williams did not produce Test form in the next two games.

Holmes played a curate's egg type of game, reminiscent of the young Gareth Edwards. Completely fearless, he killed many a loose ball. He got his usual try from a scrummage close in, but time and time again from scrummages, rucks, and mauls he used the good ball himself when he was heavily marked. They were situations which cried out for the ball to be moved to players away from the target area.

The central figure on the stage was Campbell. It was a risk to play him, a risk I would not have taken, but I had full sympathy for the management, who had a difficult decision to make, and of course Noel Murphy knew Campbell far better than anyone on this tour. Hamstrings are partly in the mind. Even Campbell himself had jocularly admitted this before the match. All eyes were upon him. His penalty, taken in the first minute, was beautifully addressed to the touchline. He sliced another, and in the thirteenth minute came the crucial test. The comparatively easy penalty attempt for him was badly fluffed as he tentatively made contact much too low on the ball. It might well have been a case of not practising kicks at goal with the aid of the sand which the ball boys always bring on to the field.

Four minutes later he kicked an easy penalty but without his usual poise and assurance. His successful effort from 45 metres in the second half was far more reassuring for the Lions, although a few minutes later he opted out of kicking from the same distance. Generally Campbell played well within himself, obviously determined not to take undue risks. He tends to cradle the ball before kicking or passing, which does not allow him the facility of setting his backs away at speed. Still he was the match-winner. Gathering a wayward ball from a shortened lineout he set off on an elusive defence-splitting run, and when he was stopped, Holmes gave to Gravell, who gave a beautiful scoring pass for Carleton.

Carleton, a minute earlier, had gone off for repairs, and according to the Africaans Press he had not sought the referee's permission to go on again. It was not a clever day for the referee, Boetie Malan of North Eastern Cape. The men of Natal felt a little cheated to have lost the game in injury time. Roger Gardner, a little disappointed, was quite philosophical. Natal had lifted their game. They gave the ball more air than the Lions, but their passing was always either static or lateral. I thought Loane was only half the player he had been, and I shall never understand why Gary Pearse, the Australian flanker, was not selected.

The prodigal Lions could have made the game safe early on. As it was they had to fight for the full eighty minutes, and into injury time for their victory. Maybe such an experience in trying conditions would benefit them more in the long run.

So far the management had made good selections. For the next game against the South African Invitation XV at Potchefstroom I thought they might show a positive hand and experiment in one or two positions. There was a question mark over the fullback, the right wing, and the open side flanker positions. It was an ideal opportunity, despite the strength of the opposition, which made one think it was another Springbok trial, to play Peter Morgan at fullback. Up to then he had played half a game at centre and half a game at outside-half. Again I would have tried Woodward on the right wing, with Richards at outside-half, and because time was short Gareth Williams I thought would have to be thrown in at the deep end.

Blakeway's Tour Ends

Monday 19 May turned out to be the most dramatic day of the tour so far. It began with Campbell pulling up during the sprints and making for Syd Millar and Jack Matthews standing on the touchline. There was no need to enquire about the nature of Campbell's injury. The bruising at the base of the hamstring told the story of the injury that had been troubling him for all but one day of the tour.

On the other side of the field Gareth Davies, his arm still in a sling, was going through some routine exercises with Phil Blakeway. The injury problems were mounting. Blakeway had not been so chirpy for the previous few days; a sure sign that the news of his rib injury was not good.

Blakeway is a most charming man. He had overcome a broken neck and various other injuries to win selection for England and for the Lions. No one was prouder to be on the tour than he, and based on his performance in the England scrum the previous season, he thoroughly deserved his place. No blame could be attached to him for wanting to make the trip, but the fact was that he should not have been allowed to go. His injury was an old one received during England's match against France in February. Against Wales and against Scotland he had played with pain-killing injections, and anyone who saw him during the latter stages of the Calcutta Cup match could have deduced that the man was suffering agonies.

It might have been wise at that time to have taken X-rays of Blakeway's ribs, although he had been fully examined twice before then and no evidence was found of the rib fracture which on this fateful Monday was going to take eight to ten weeks to repair. For Blakeway, like Lane, the tour was over. Both would be returning home after the first Test.

A replacement would also be required at outside-half, for neither Campbell nor Davies was likely to be fit for the Test. The most obvious choice was Tony Ward, who lost his place to Campbell in the Ireland side. Ward could kick goals, but there were dark tales that Murphy would not have him at any price as he considered him to be too selfish a player. That may have been so, although it was worth bearing in mind that the Irish threequarter line outside Ward was of such poor quality that he was probably right to take matters into his own hands. Be that as it may, desperate circumstances called for desperate measures, and whatever the feelings of Murphy and Millar may have been towards Ward, they had to take second place to the more pressing needs of the moment.

Ward was sent for, and so was the Bridgend prop, Ian Stephens, a Wales B international, to replace Blakeway. Stephens was touring in Canada with the Wales B side at the time. One wondered what Wales B made of it all, having lost Williams the week before. No doubt however Rod Morgan, chairman of the Welsh selectors, and John Lloyd, the Welsh coach, both Bridgend men, would be delighted to lose two of their club's players for the cause of the Lions.

Had it not been for a change in the tours agreement which allowed the Tourists to supplement the party, the Lions would have been in very serious trouble. Under the old system the touring side could have a maximum of thirty players, but under the new agreement a party could be supplemented by 'a reasonable number of replacements', who would be paid for in this case by the Four Home Unions. The Lions could therefore keep Campbell and Davies with them, which in the latter stages of the tour might be of the greatest benefit. In fact Davies went home a month before the end of the tour.

The training session in Durban gave Gareth Williams the first chance to stretch his legs. He had arrived the previous Saturday having been held up for twenty-four hours at Las Palmas. He looked in good shape and it was encouraging to notice he was quite tall. He was paired with Beattie in the sprints and came off second best, so Beattie remained the fastest member of the back row in the absence of Lane. The selectors obviously intended to persevere with Beattie, who received instruction from Murphy on the finer arts of loose forward play. But he was moved from No. 8 to the side of the scrum, a position he had never occupied before. The Scots were getting a lot of instruction. Beaumont and Quinnell went to great lengths to help Alan Tomes place his feet correctly in the scrum.

The team selected for Potchefstroom turned out to be much the same as the previous Wednesday side, although it was strengthened by Saturday players like Slemen, Price, and Richards, who would have his second match at outside-half, his third game in a row. Morgan was not in, and it was a mystery what the management planned for him. He had been inactive since the first game of the tour. Gareth Williams was booked for his first match.

The Invitation XV was one of almost Test strength; in fact many people labelled the match the 'mid-week Test'. Whatever the management thought of these 'loaded' mid-week sides they kept it to themselves, but if they were to face opponents of this calibre the Lions' chances of going through unbeaten were slim.

Adding insult to injury the Invitation XV spent the Monday before the match practising at Loftus Versfeldt with the Springbok side who had beaten the Jaguars in their second Test. That was the South African Board's way of getting round the thorny subject of squad sessions. They called it an extra trial. That had been a most productive day for them, especially the Invitation XV, who had out-scrummaged their opponents. In their scrum they had Willie Kahts, who was later to be selected as hooker for the Newlands Test against the Lions, a prop, Martiens le Roux, and a lock, de Villiers Visser, both of whom had toured Britain with the South African Barbarians. Alongside de Villiers Visser in the second row was Moaner van Heerden, who was well known to the 1974 Lions, and who also was later to win a Springbok place. In the back row were Thys Burger, who had played so well in the match at East London, and Wynand Claassen, the Natal captain. Behind the scrum were the Western Province pair, Divan Serfontein, another who later played in the Springbok side, and Robbie Blair at half-back. In the centre were David Smith, a most exciting player from Zimbabwe who also got his Test place, and Hennie Shields, a Cape Coloured man who had toured with the Barbarians. At that time Shields was reckoned to be the man most likely to make Rugby history by being the first non-white man to play in the Springbok side.

The original 1980 British Lions party just before they left London: *Left to right, back row*: Colin Patterson, David Richards, Peter Morgan, Clive Woodward, Ollie Campbell, Mike Slemen, Stuart Lane, Alan Phillips, Elgan Rees, Rodney O'Donnell, Jim Renwick. *Middle row*: Gareth Davies, Terry Holmes, John Beattie, Alan Tomes, Allan Martin, Ray Gravell, Maurice Colclough, John O'Driscoll, Colm Tucker, John Carleton, Phil Blakeway. *Front row*: Dr J. Matthews (Team doctor), Graham Price, Bruce Hay, Fran Cotton, Syd Millar (Manager), Bill Beaumont (Captain), Noel Murphy (Assistant Manager), Derek Quinnell, Peter Wheeler, Jeff Squire, Clive Williams.

The making of history: Bruce Hay gives the final pass to Mike Slemen who is about to score the epic try at Potchefstroom. Divan Serfontein, (9) the Springbok scrum-half fails to stop them.

Happy Birthday trio: On Friday 23 May Syd Millar, David Richards, and Bruce Hay celebrated their birthdays. Millar was 46, Richards 26, and Hay 30.

John O'Driscoll wins a short lineout against Orange Free State at Bloemfontein.

LEFT ABOVE Fran Cotton leaves the field at Stellenbosch holding his chest. LEFT BELOW David Richards in pain as he goes off at Johannesburg with a dislocated shoulder. It was the end of the tour for both Lions.

ABOVE Victor of the hunt: Bill Beaumont displays the kudu he shot near Windhoek.

RIGHT ABOVE Smiles at Stellenbosch: Syd Millar and Nellie Smith, the Springboks coach, watch the Lions train for the South African Federation match, and RIGHT BELOW Cape Coloured fans cheer the mixed white and coloured Federation side.

Another day, another game: Ollie Campbell hits one of his 32 runs for the Lions Players and Press against the Springboks.

8
Great Moment in Rugby History

The 23,000 people who packed the Olen Stadium at Potchef-stroom on 21 May, 1980, were privileged to witness one of the truly great moments in Rugby history, when the Lions achieved what surely must be one of the most magnificent try-scoring movements in the long saga of the game. Five minutes remained, and the Lions were 16–19 down to this shadow Springbok side, playing as a South African Invitation XV. Then David Richards, who had played with little conviction, shook off the indifference which appeared to have settled on him, and ran from his own twenty-two straight through the opposition defence into their half of the field. Five rucks, thirty-three pairs of hands, and 1 minute 45 seconds later, Mike Slemen scored the try.

There were times when it seemed impossible that anything could come from the seemingly endless twisting and turning of the Lions' running, and the marvel of it was that somehow or other they kept running. Each time a Lion showed signs of breaking through, a defender was there to pull him down, and once the Invitation side even managed to drive the Lions back over the halfway line. But the Lions restarted from every checkpoint, and as they began running again so the crowd's excitement grew. For friend or foe it was a wonderful sight to watch.

Chick Henderson, who had played so much of his Rugby in Britain, was relaying the spectacle to South African Broadcasting Corporation listeners. He must have established a record for continuous commentary. This is how he described the amazing happenings:

'The lineout is on the far side of the field on the Lions' 22

... that is on the Lions' right ... Willie Kahts with the throw, but it's palmed back by John O'Driscoll ... Patterson does well to clean up there, and passes out to Richards who has some room to move ... a lively run by him ... he has broken the defence, up now to the 10 metre line ... Richards is held, but there is Gareth Williams in support, O'Driscoll too is with him ... the tackle comes in from David Smith and we have a ruck 20 metres in from the Lions' right ... the ball comes back on the Lions' side to Patterson, who puts Richards away on the left, and Richards misses Woodward giving straight to Slemen ... again it's Smith who is first with the tackle on the Invitation 22, but Bruce Hay is there ... Hay tackled by Serfontein, and now into a ruck ... Williams manages to work the ball back just outside the Invitation 22 and this time the Lions are going right to Woodward ... on to Quinnell, to Renwick, and now on the right wing to Elgan Rees ... Rees checks, comes inside over the 22, but is held up ... there is Quinnell, in there again working the ball back to Patterson ... he switches left to Richards, now Woodward ... Woodward cuts right, now he is coming left, tackled by Tim Nkonki ... the ball goes loose, picked up by Slemen, and he passes inside to Williams ... now it is his turn to be held up, and again the ball is free. At last the white shirt gets to it first, it's Nkonki, he fly-kicks down the field, back into the Lions' half ... Richards is back there ... tries to get it away to Woodward, but it's Renwick who picks it up ... he goes left, darts right over the half-way line ... the Lions are on the attack again ... when will it end? ... now Phillips gets in on the action ... he twists and feeds Patterson. Patterson to Rees, Rees back infield, stopped by van Heerden just outside the Invitation 22 ... The ruck forms, and again it comes back on the Lions' side to Patterson. From Patterson to Richards, to Renwick, to Woodward ... and coming up outside Woodward is Bruce Hay, who drives through Hennie Shields' tackle and gives the ball to Slemen, who has come up on the inside ... Slemen has just Claassen to beat ... he's going to score. I just don't believe it.'

At the end of it all there was a stunned silence. Players lay about the field in various stages of exhaustion. It was uncanny. Gradually the players picked themselves up from the ground, dazed, as if in slow motion. It seemed an age for the wonder of this spectacle to sink into one's mind. Then almost as one, the whole crowd rose, their loyalties and prejudices forgotten in those glorious moments, as they acknowledged with thunderous sound this greatest of tries, and when at last they became quiet, Woodward, barely able to swing his leg at the ball from in front of the goal – Slemen had scored between the posts – somehow lifted it over the bar.

One was thankful for the modern aids of radio and film to help reconstruct this amazing piece of play, even if they could not completely recapture the tremendously thrilling emotions of the spectators while it was all happening. Several viewings of the film afterwards established that eleven different Lions had taken part in the handling, some of them several times of course.

Quinnell, captain for the day, galloped about the field as if he were the embodiment of a demented soul, but he accomplished, in chasing his men from ruck to ruck, as much as anyone in keeping the movement alive. The memory of pieces of continuous play that have occurred over the years is perhaps a little dimmed, and no-one seems to have timed any such effort in days gone by, so that this amazing incident at Potchefstroom may well have created a record for play without a stoppage.

So the Lions, as they had done in Durban, had left it uncomfortably late to achieve victory. Perhaps too much of their early effort had gone in the forwards battle, which was hard in the extreme, although perfectly fair, but they held out for the remaining few minutes after Slemen's try to win their fourth match in a row.

Praise for Patterson

by Carwyn James

The try, which will of course always be remembered, was similar in style to the one scored by J.P.R. Williams for the Barbarians against the All Blacks in 1973 or the try scored by Alan Richards for Llanelli against Dawie de Villiers' Springboks in 1970 when the ball passed through twenty-three pairs of hands and three rucks. Perhaps the try hid the fact that it was only on a couple of other occasions the Lions spun the ball. From a wheeled scrummage which put the opposing back row in no man's land on the narrow side, Patterson sent Richards away at speed. He had missed out Renwick for Woodward to slip his man and Hay was the linkman for Slemen's try.

Patterson played a gem of a game. His service off the ground was like lightning; he took the right options, and he was very much lieutenant to Quinnell, marshalling and inspiring the troops.

On this tour however the sheer physical presence of Terry Holmes was needed. He had strength at the set pieces, his tackling was fierce and fearless, and he had the ability to play a flanker's game as well. The Lions were fortunate to have two such competent scrum-halves. Woodward played to a high standard, but he missed a couple of tackles in opposition to David Smith, the strong Zimbabwe centre, who scored the Invitation side's only try. Later Smith was in the Springboks' side for the first Test. After this game I still felt that Woodward would be better employed on the right wing. His place-kicking had been a revelation and of course a match-winning factor.

In the second minute of the match there was an interesting confrontation between Quinnell and van Heerden, who I remembered had been accused of stamping on Peter Whiting's ear in the third Test in 1976. That was a thoroughly nasty incident which incensed the New Zealanders when it was shown there on television. Quinnell and van Heerden snarled at one another but got on with the game.

In fact all the games so far had been whiter than snow, despite many frustrating decisions by referees. Quinnell was proving to be a superb leader of the midweek side, and that onerous but worthwhile task would not keep him out of the Test side if he maintained that form. Colclough was struck a savage blow early on, whether by accident or design I was not sure, but it certainly spurred him to much greater deeds than he had achieved at East London. He gave a performance worthy of Test recognition, and if Beaumont was not the captain I would have played Martin and Colclough in the first Test. Gareth Williams started well, then he had a quiet period before finishing strongly. His presence at the tail of the lineout was significant, while Thys Burger was not so prominent as he had been for SARA. O'Driscoll played a lively game. It was his deflection which initiated Slemen's memorable try.

The Lions lost the lineouts by two to one, but they were much quicker on the loose ball, and they easily won the mauls and the rucks. Price, although accused in the Press, both Afrikaans and British, of collapsing the scrums, gave his opposite number van der Merwe, a huge unathletic hulk of a man, a most uncomfortable afternoon.

Robbie Blair, the Invitation outside-half, was a fine kicker of the ball, but as a pivot he was sadly lacking in the basics of the game. His passing was so ponderous that he completely failed to get his line moving at speed, which hampered the activities of Smith and Shields in the centre, and the full-back incursions of Cox. At the end of the game, with only a minute or two to go, Blair tried to drop a goal instead of passing the ball along the line. He was going for a draw and not for victory. Then at the very end when Cox had the ball and should have been running – any schoolboy would have done that – he passed the ball back to another player in support who put the ball into touch. It was typical of the negative thinking of this side. Shields was a courageous tackler but he failed to show any attacking form, so his chance of being the first coloured man to play for the Springboks became rather slim.

At the Lions' hotel after the match there was one very nasty and unpleasant incident, when some local white 'yobos' were taunting Shields and saying that 'if the black bastards had not been playing the Invitation side would have beaten the Lions.' Stuart Lane and David Richards were there with one or two other Lions, and they were most incensed at this kind of arrogance. It was fortunate that the affair did not come to blows, as it very nearly did.

Even from the Press one realized that the South African selectors, who were choosing their Test team that night, had a crisis on their hands. Ian Kirkpatrick, one of the selectors, was to have taken Ollie Campbell back to the Sports Clinic in Johannesburg, but Campbell was told that he would have to make other arrangements because it was going to be a very very long meeting. Obviously the Springbok selectors had been placed in much disarray because their second Springbok side had not done so well as they thought they would. In fact, on the following Saturday, when they were going to settle the team finally, the selectors split their forces, and only three of the six watched the Lions game in Bloemfontein. The other three went to a Currie Cup game between Natal and Western Province, and a match between Boland and Northern Free State.

So far as the Lions' Test team was concerned one had to remember that a major tour is judged not on the results of the provincial matches but on winning the Test series. The Lions of 1968 had lost to Transvaal and they drew one Test match. Ivan Vodanovich's All Blacks of 1970 had a brilliant provincial record only to lose the series, and the same fate befell J.J. Stewart's All Blacks in 1976. The Lions of 1974 were unbeaten. Every selection is carefully weighed and analysed in the nervous build-up to the first Test. On every tour some players are 'more equal than others'. The gold are given Saturday contracts, the silver play on Tuesday or Wednesday, while the bronze, and there are only one or two of those, are protected. The midweek and Saturday pattern usually emerges before the first Test, by which time the experiment of the various permutations will have been tried.

In the Bloemfontein match against Orange Free State Peter

Morgan was at last brought into the Lions side at fullback, but maybe that was too late for him to make a challenge to Rodney O'Donnell for the Test place. Still Morgan would have brought another dimension because he loves running at the opposition, and having seen that brilliant try at Potchefstroom I thought the Lions needed to counter-attack. Slemen, an outstanding all-round footballer, would play on the left wing, but for one reason or another neither John Carleton nor Elgan Rees had been entirely convincing. I still would have put Woodward on the right wing. In the centre I would have had Gravell to complement the smooth elusive running of Richards, and in the absence of Campbell and Davies, although Richards had comfortably occupied the outside-half position, Tony Ward, who had arrived in Bloemfontein two days before the Orange Free State match; I thought he would probably be the Test pivot and the No. 1 place-kicker.

The diminutive scrum-half Colin Patterson having played a gem of a game at Potchefstroom, so different from his fussy first performance in South Africa, I thought Ward might prefer to reform his international partnership with his Irish colleague. I had a feeling though that Terry Holmes might win the Test place, as he might have done if he and Davies had been fit when the selection was made.

Undoubtedly the Lions selectors would have liked the experience of Cotton, Wheeler, and Price to make a formidable front row, but Cotton was out of it by the time the Test selection came. I thought Martin would ride the challenge of Colclough in the second row, but he did not. Squire and Quinnell picked themselves, but the open side was anyone's guess. In fact O'Driscoll won the place, although I would have put him behind Tucker and Gareth Williams in order of choice.

As I saw it at that time, there would no doubt be changes in the Springbok team, which looked ponderous and unimaginative against the more lively Jaguars. Pierre Edwards, the fullback, was carried off suffering from concussion early in the second half, and the man who took his place, Gysie Pienaar, looked a much better prospect. We could expect a change in the centre, for David Smith, who scored against the Lions at Potchefstroom, must gain his first cap, and Willie Kahts would be the new hooker. I thought van Heerden would challenge strongly for a place at lock and he succeeded, and I thought Louw and Stofberg might lose their flank places, but they did not.

The first Test then was about as evenly poised as any confrontation could be. Having a neutral referee was an excellent idea, and a French interpretation of the law should not frighten the Lions. Nothing should frighten a team capable of scoring the type of try we saw at Potchefstroom!

9
Pienaar
Pleases

When the Lions arrived at Bloemfontein after a three-hour bus journey from Potchefstroom, they found for once that they were not front page news. The lead story made grisly reading. There had been riots, bombings, and general mayhem in the streets of Bethel, a black township on the outskirts of Bloemfontein. Schoolchildren were roaming the streets in hordes, and the disturbances were all part of the dissatisfaction concerning the alleged inferior education of black children. For a time there was a boycott of schools, which later had been lifted. There were many who thought the boycott should continue, and this led to intimidation of children who had ignored the boycott call. Some people thought it was not pure coincidence that the riots should have broken out when the Lions were in town. The Lions saw nothing of the violence, but it was proof of the tension that existed in South Africa. Violence on the Rugby field had so far been absent from the encounters, which had been physically hard but fair.

In Bloemfontein the Lions were to play Orange Free State. The problems the Lions had been having at full-back persuaded them that at last it was time to try Peter Morgan in that position. They were beginning to regret the absence of an attacking full-back, which in South Africa, where the ball was continually hoofed far up field by opposing backs, meant that they were being denied many golden opportunities of counter-attacking. Could Peter Morgan be the answer? He was well aware of the importance of the action, and that the time had come for him to specialize in one position. He was in great danger of being penalised for his versatility. The week before he was due to play outside-half for Wales against Ireland, his club, Llanelli, had played him in the centre. It was grossly unfair to ask a player to keep changing positions and expect him to produce a level of competence in keeping with the standard at which he was playing.

Maurice Colclough was another who stood to gain much from a good display. At Potchefstroom he had played with a vigour which had been entirely missing from his play the week before at East London. The question, with the Test in mind, was whether the selectors could sacrifice strength for the superior lineout skill of Allan Martin. The outside-half position was clouded by injuries to Gareth Davies and Ollie Campbell, and the Test choice lay between David Richards and Tony Ward, who could not play at Bloemfontein because he arrived there only the day before the match. Richards was to play at Bloemfontein, his third game at outside-half. He had not given the impression that he enjoyed it, but if the Lions were hellbent on attack then he had to be the man. Of course without Ward in the Test the Lions would be without a goal-kicker of proven ability at international level. Even if a place were to be found for Clive Woodward, who had astonished everyone, including himself, by his success at goal-kicking, it would be too much of a risk to burden him with the duties of principal goal-kicker in a Test. In fact things worked out more easily than seemed possible at this stage, for Richards played in the centre and Ward was at outside-half in the Test.

The Free State had a huge pack including a couple of vast locks, Vries Visagie, who is 6 foot 7 inches and wears size fifteen boots, and Klippe Kritzinger, who weighs all of eighteen stones, and who had turned out for the Springboks at flank forward. In the front row was Martiens le Roux renewing his acquaintance with Clive Williams, whom he had played against at Potchefstroom. Le Roux was at tight-head in the Springbok side in the first Test the following week, and Gysie Pienaar, the full-back, also won his Test place. As if they were not enough, de Wet Ras, the outside-half, proved to be the longest goal-kicker the Lions had met up to then.

The Lions had not been spared the banter of the local pundits and were by then well aware that their predecessors six years before had won this match only in injury time. Of course for the 1980 Lions that would not be a new experience.

There was very little about the match that could have pleased the management, coming as it did a week before the Test. Terry Holmes took a terrible pounding all through from the Free State loose forwards, and eventually left the field holding his shoulder, much as Davies had done three weeks previously. With David Richards failing to show the sort of control necessary at outside-half the Lions backs were able to make very little of the possession gained by the forwards. It was a pity because the forwards gave what was probably their best show of the tour so far.

One of the worst features of the game was the line kicking which for the most part was wretchedly off course. Even Mike Slemen, normally so accurate, missed time and again, although he made up for these failures by scoring two tries, bringing his total to five in four matches. With a strong wind behind him in the first half de Wet Ras made the Lions pay for their careless-ness. Fortunately for the Tourists he was not so accurate with his goal-kicking, and before he went off with an injury similar to the one Holmes had, he had missed with three kicks, one certainly being from sixty-five metres. That act of bravado up-staged the Lions kicker for the day, Jin Renwick, who was no more successful from less daunting distances. In all he missed seven out of nine attempts.

The Free State led 7–0 at half-time with a penalty goal by Pienaar and a try by Derek Jeffrey after a glorious sixty metres run. With the wind advantage the Lions took only two minutes to score in the second half. Holmes broke away from the front of a lineout and scored his third try in as many matches. From the touchline Renwick kicked the goal. Slemen's try, the second after some nifty footwork by Renwick, caused some complac-ency in the Lions' ranks, and this was exploited by the Free State captain Barry Woolmarans. His try spurred the Lions to a further flurry of activity, Wheeler stealing a try after some slackness by the Free State at the lineout, and Renwick at last kicked a penalty goal.

This should have made the game safe but for some inexplicable reason Richards, with five minutes to go, decided to run from inside his own 22. Down went the ball, and despite protestations from Morgan, who felt he had won the touchdown over Danie Gerber, a try was awarded and Pienaar converted. So again the Lions were left to sweat it out for the last few minutes, a ludicrous position for them to be in with the amount of possession they had had.

Carwyn James comments:

It was de Wet Ras who reminded us, if we needed reminding, that we were playing in the rarified atmosphere of the High Veldt. His first shot at goal was from sixty-five or seventy metres. Fortunately for the Lions it was a little wide and a little short, and he missed a couple of others as well. But his long punting meant that Morgan, playing only his second game of the tour, and this time at fullback, had to station himself at seventy metres from the kicker. It was a most unpleasant experience for him; like a small boy running round the boundary, he sometimes got a hand to the ball, he fumbled a few, and one or two went over his head.

Shortly before half-time Ray Gravell made contact with de Wet Ras. It was a late tackle; it laid the victim out, and he was taken off the field. I would not say that it was a deliberate late tackle, but even Gravell's greatest fans would have to admit that it was ill-timed. When reprimanded about it jocularly by the management Gravell's response was 'I got there as fast as I could'. In a country where the tiniest molehill, if written about in the local and national papers, assumes the proportions of Table Mountain, it was amazing how quiet the native scribes were about this incident. Probably it was being stocked in the bank for a rainy day when a Springbok might transgress likewise.

Morgan had a much better second half and seemed so glad to be able to take a real part in the game that he almost knocked himself out in a crunching tackle on Jeffrey, the strong running left wing, but on the whole Morgan did not play well, and except for Holmes and Slemen, neither did any of the backs. Richards lacked the control which produces the rhythmic three-quarter flow, and his line kicking was wayward. Pienaar was grateful for the tiniest of offerings, and again he showed that he was capable of playing the counter-attacking game. Obviously the four Springbok selectors present were pleased with his performance, for that night they chose him for the first Test. Gerber in the centre played strongly and posed many problems for Gravell and Renwick, probably because the alignment of the Lions centres was all wrong. Renwick had the added responsibility of kicking at goal and as he missed so often the Lions made heavy weather of defeating an inferior combination. At this level place-kicking is of great importance.

Slemen had another pleasing game and Holmes's try on the narrow side from the lineout sticks in the memory. Sadly though the injury jinx hit the Lions again, this time Holmes being the victim.

The forwards gave another strong performance and Colclough made sure that the lock position and the middle of the lineout jumper spot for the Test was his.

That the Lions were winning without playing well as a team was encouraging, but looking ahead then to the first Test, one wondered whether they would continue to get away with it. Much work had to be done with the backs.

Springbok Selection

Pienaar, who won his Springbok place after the Free State game, had gone on for Pierre Edwards as a replacement in the second international against South America. Martiens le Roux was one of four new caps. The others were David Smith, the Zimbabwe centre, Divan Serfontein the scrum-half, and the hooker Willie

Kahts. All four had played in the Invitation XV at Potchefstroom, but it was a surprise that the selectors had included Serfontein, a most talented player with a fast accurate pass and a good break. Was it a sign that the Springboks were intending to expand their hitherto limited game?

The Sunday after the Free State game was a long day for the Lions. Because of student unrest in Cape Town it was decided to alter the travelling arrangements, and by 7.30 a.m. the Lions had decamped. The decision had been taken by the South African Rugby Board, who thought that the students might want to make political capital out of the Lions' arrival. The day before about 3,000 Cape Coloured students had poured into the main shopping centre in the city, causing widespread disruption. There were baton charges by the police and more than 100 arrests. The students were protesting about the closure of the University of the Western Cape, the handling of the meat-workers' strike, and the threatened closure of certain schools, the pupils of which were continuing their pursuit of the boycott.

The demonstrations brought to mind the problems encountered by the 1976 All Blacks, when Ian Kirkpatrick and several other players were actually caught up in the maelstrom and had to be rescued by the police. There were no such incidents this time, but the police took no chances. Throughout the Lions' stay the hotel was constantly patrolled by some very young looking policemen, described with a suitable sense of drama by the players as 'a ring of steel'.

The only sign of unrest that appeared personally to any of the players occurred on the day before the Test when Ollie Campbell and Tony Ward went to the grounds of Cape Town University to practise their kicking. There they were barracked by a group of about a hundred or so Cape Coloured youths who had gone into the grounds from outside – there are no coloured students at the University. Two of them ran on to the field and said 'We want you to leave'. Rather than cause any more trouble Campbell and Ward picked up the ball and walked off. Both were slightly upset by it, but there was no violence.

It was as well the Lions were spared any further presence of demonstrators because they had more than enough troubles of their own.

Fran Cotton, who had not been looking at all well at Potchefstroom, rejoined the party for the game at Bloemfontein accompanied by his most solicitous escort Phil Blakeway. If Cotton was to play in the Test then he would have to prove his fitness in the mid-week match against the South African Rugby Federation at Stellenbosch. As events turned out it was the very last thing he should have done. Holmes appeared on the Sunday night with his arm in a sling; he had strained shoulder ligaments and would be out for two or three weeks. Surely there had to be a limit to the Lions' bad luck!

There was one piece of good fortune, though. John Robbie of Ireland, the official reserve for the scrum-half position, was at that time playing for the Goshawks in Zimbabwe, and he was therefore able to join the Lions. They could not possibly go into a Test without specialist cover, and Robbie was the obvious choice. The plan was that he would stay only for as long as he was required and would then return home. It was a perfectly permissable arrangement under the new tour agreement which allowed a touring team to supplement its playing strength in case of undue stress. If any team had been under stress it was this one.

Robbie was the fourth replacement to arrive in three weeks; and that was a record. With five caps, he is a player of considerable class. He had captained Cambridge University, and he was surely being thought of as a future captain of Ireland. Furthermore his ability as a place-kicker would be of benefit to the Lions. So there were four Irish half-backs in the party, equalling the record set by Wales in 1977 when they supplied all four half-backs in New Zealand. A final bonus was that Robbie was, of course, match fit.

10
Stellenbosch Sadness

In preparation for their sixth match against the South African Rugby Federation, the Lions made the thirty-mile coach trip from Cape Town to Stellenbosch, the home of Danie Craven, to train. For the first time on the tour they trained in torrential rain, which had a certain novelty value. In the conditions the standard of handling was fairly good. Tony Ward, who was to play his first game, fitted well into the scheme of things, and moved smoothly on to Colin Patterson's service from the base of the scrum. His goal-kicking practice at the end of the session was equally impressive. He went about it with an air of efficiency and a sense of purpose beginning from in front of the posts and finishing out on the touchline.

The next day was an historic one for the University of Stellenbosch. It was the first time that an international touring team had played at Stellenbosch since W.E. Maclagan's British side had what they delightfully called a 'picnic game' there in 1891, which they did not count in the official record of their tour. There was a very apt descriptive report in the *Cape Argus* of Monday 7 September 1891 which recalled the scene at Stellenbosch shortly before the match. This is an extract:

Stellenbosch is in holiday garb today and all the countryside and his wife are in town. Hundreds are arriving in carts from the Paarl and the suburbs. The excitement is over the visit of the English team who arrived here by special train this morning, and will play a Stellenbosch team this afternoon. On arrival at Bosman's Crossing the team was received by Mr Kriege MLA, and carts being in waiting, the vehicles were

driven to Mr Roux's farm at Vredenburg and then around
the town. At one o'clock luncheon took place in the Victoria
College Hall. At half past six the teams will be privately dined
at the Royal, and at ten tonight everyone will go home. The
English team, notwithstanding their rough handling, look
extremely fit. The countrymen are a strong lot and are
confident of winning. The general opinion however, is that
England will give an exhibition of loose play. The day is
gloriously fine, the trees are clothed in green verger, and the
visitors are enjoying themselves to their hearts' content.

Eighty-nine years on, the day was gloriously fine, the trees wore
autumn colours, and there had been few more beautiful settings
than the Danie Craven Stadium at Stellenbosch. The only
unfortunate thing was that the visitors were certainly not
enjoying themselves to their hearts' content. The Lions had
chosen a side containing at least nine Test possibles. It was a
selection forced upon the management by injuries, and a natural
shrewdness in not wishing to declare their hand and their
strength. Again the mid-week side had been 'loaded'.

The Federation side, playing under the name of Proteas, had
decided, because of the decline in their standards, to call in the
Western Province front five forwards, one of whom, Hempies
du Toit, had been left out of the Test side in favour of le Roux,
and had a point to prove to the Springbok selectors. He went
about his job with a certain relish. His confrontation with Fran
Cotton bordered on the savage, and it was no surprise to see
Cotton leave the field mid-way through the first half holding his
chest. Even he failed to appreciate the seriousness of his complaint. The whole thing was an inglorious mess, which prompted
Syd Millar to say afterwards, 'The Stadium here was named after
a great man, the setting was idyllic, but today I have seen some
things that I never want to see repeated. I was very disappointed.'

The Lions had no need to become involved in anything
unsavoury. They began well enough with John Carleton scoring
a try which Tony Ward converted from the touchline. It was a
comforting sight for the Lions, who minutes earlier had watched

their goal-kicking hope miss from twenty-five metres. The day was not a happy one for Ward, though; he missed with six attempts out of nine. The Lions held their own in the lineout, but when Hennie Becker and de Villiers Visser began to win the ball in the middle of the lineout, each succeeding scrummage formed with greater ferocity.

At this stage the referee, Dr Gouws, should have made his thoughts perfectly clear; that he did not was sad for the players, the spectators, and for Rugby. The Lions lost their rhythm, and the game developed into a bruising maul by the forwards, punctuated by some of the worst back play seen from the Lions in a long time. By half-time the Lions were leading 9–3, O'Donnell having dropped a goal and Tobias having kicked a penalty goal. The second half was a repetition of the first, only slightly more bellicose, with several fist fights erupting. Ward kicked two penalties, and Tobias another for the Federation.

There was no doubt that had the Federation side been better organized they could quite easily have won the match. Fortunately for the Lions, Tobias was not at his best, and the carelessness of the Federation backs was if anything even more culpable than that of the Lions. To be sure the Lions were bad enough. There were times when Patterson looked as if he had never seen Ward before; when David Richards looked as if he had never heard of the term 'alignment', and when no-one looked to be a player of international class. Only O'Donnell could have been happy with his display. He was fearless in the most testing circumstances, and hardly put a foot wrong. His Test place was certain.

The lasting feeling though was one of sadness. The setting had been, as Millar said, idyllic, and the opposition had been put up as further evidence of progress along the road to multi-racial sport. There was in truth, though, very little about the play that in any way resembled progress in sport.

Carwyn James elaborates on this:

Of course we all felt sad, because the situation had been so right for a beautiful game. The weather was absolutely perfect. It had rained the day before, but the match day was lovely. The Welsh Youth had played magnificently in the curtain-raiser, and they were refereed by Francis Palmade. Some Welsh supporters had arrived, and as I looked at the the ground, a beautiful ground, with fields in the background, it reminded me of many of the beautiful scenes painted by Captain Williams, one of the best known Welsh painters.

But the game itself was dreadful. I often use two Greek words, 'arete' meaning winning by playing beautiful Rugby, and 'hubris' meaning winning at all costs.

Here was a good example of 'hubris'. I think the front five from Western Province gave the confidence to the coloured players to play that kind of game; there were so many late tackles, and so much obstruction.

When Millar came off the field he met Cuthbert Loriston, President of the Cape Coloured, who said 'What a great game!' Millar replied 'That was one of the worst games I have ever seen, and I don't want to see a repetition of it. It happened in 1974, and if you carry on like this, well, your Union is going to suffer a great deal.'

Unfortunately the same theme continued in the evening. When we got to the lovely town centre – and what a magnificent hall it was – the Mayor made a speech, which he had obviously prepared a week or two before, because he said that it was a marvellous game and he had thoroughly enjoyed it. Of course it had been nothing of the kind. Cuthbert Loriston had obviously changed his speech by that time. He tried to make a claim that mayhem was a part of Rugby football; a feature of the game which was acceptable. It was, I think, a stupid speech.

Syd Millar said, 'On this occasion I am blaming the selectors. If they pick the wrong men to play this kind of Rugby then they are to blame for the ugly side of the game. I hope I do not see any more instances of it on this tour.' Millar had told his players on more than one occasion, 'There will be no violence on this tour.' They all knew he meant it, and thought he was quite right.

By the time this after-match function took place, Bill Beaumont had gone to see Cotton in hospital, and for the first time on the tour the captain for the day, Derek Quinnell, was allowed to make the speech. He is quite a good after-dinner speaker, and he thanked the opposition for a good game, 'a lovely game', he said, but added ominously, 'We look forward to meeting some of these players again'. This was a direct reference to the Western Province front five. I don't know whether Quinnell ought to have made such a pointed comment – the inference was that it would be a pretty hot game next time – but it was his way of disagreeing with the kind of Rugby that had been played that afternoon.

Another Replacement

Beaumont's absence from the after-match function caused some whispers. His visit to Cotton in hospital was a sure sign that his old Lancashire pal was rather more poorly than the management made out. Rumours spread that Cotton was having respiratory problems. What was not known was that he had been given an ECG when he came off the field, and that it had been positive.

It was a very subdued party that trooped the next morning into the team room to hear the announcement of the side for the first Test. There was no more charming man on the tour than Cotton, and the thought that his Rugby career might now be over was a terrible blow to a team who had already suffered more than their share of misfortune.

On the Wednesday morning when the Lions went to Newlands to train, Millar officially announced what everybody had by then deduced, that Cotton had suffered a mild coronary, and had been transferred from Stellenbosch to Cape Town, that he was as well as could be expected, and that his Rugby career was in all probability over. With the advantage of hindsight one

could be clear that Cotton should not have played at Stellenbosch. The previous week at Potchefstroom he had complained
to Noel Murphy during a training session that he had a pain in
his chest which caused him the greatest difficulty in breathing.
Thinking it was merely the effect of the altitude, Murphy
encouraged him to do another lap of the field, but when Cotton
felt no better he was immediately advised to rest. This he did,
but he went back later in the session apparently none the worse.
That night Cotton felt dreadful. It was the start of his inflamed
varicose veins for which he was put on a course of antibiotics.
It seemed to account for his difficulties that morning. During
the game at Stellenbosch Cotton again complained of chest
pains, this time to Allan Martin, and Martin gave him the best
possible advice. 'Get off the field right now.' By Thursday lunchtime the party was in better spirits. The initial tests on Cotton
had shown him to be suffering from inflammation of the heart,
possibly brought on by the antibiotics, and not a coronary.
Anyway Phil Orr, the experienced prop who had played twenty-
four times for Ireland, was on his way to replace Cotton. Noel
Murphy had an agonizing thought that in some way he had
been responsible for Cotton's trouble. He had not, of course,
but he had aged a year in the minutes that he had spent with
Cotton before the ambulance had taken him to the hospital in
Stellenbosch.

Test Choice

The team announced for the first Test was: O'Donnell; Carleton,
Renwick, Richards, Slemen; Ward, Patterson; Clive Williams,
Wheeler, Price, Colclough, Beaumont, O'Driscoll, Squire,
Quinnell.

The playing tactic is to take on the foe where he is strongest,
and the strength of South African Rugby over the years has been

impeccable scrummaging. That fact was much appreciated by Millar, who was in South Africa as a Lion in 1962 and 1968. Millar the prop, a master craftsman of the loose and tight head sides, returned in 1974 as Millar the coach, and he did the brave thing. He took the Springbok by the horns and rendered him as strong as a hairless Samson.

Millar the manager, like Craven, believed that the scrummage was the most important part of the game because it was a predictable mechanical drill to be taught and learned as part of the physical contact sport. Nowhere is the contact more demanding than in the organized huddle of sixteen men each doing a specialist job.

'An understanding of the contribution made by each forward is so important,' said Millar. 'I want all my forwards to know why they should scrummage well.' So he argued that the contribution must be positive in making the opposition defensive and creating more space for your own backs. If the front five do the donkey work properly there is every chance that the middle, or the pivot five, can get on with the more creative side of the tactical game, thereby releasing the potential of the threequarters and fullback. It is a sad fact of life that in international Rugby these days we see little of the third five.

It was clearly written on the cards that in the first Test Naas Botha would not entrust the ball to anyone, but keep it for his own right boot. Millar's policy therefore of pressurizing and putting the opposition on the defensive was the right one. He and Noel Murphy had selected a scrummaging eight. Colclough was a stronger scrummager than Martin; and Martin was a better lineout practitioner than Colclough. But as Murphy said, 'You can dispute the lineout much more easily, a little nudge here, another there; even the weather can spoil your better efforts.' Not so the scrummage, which relies entirely on technique for quality possession. The keystone is a loose-head prop who must be strong and short of back to be able to withstand the natural swing of the scrum towards him. Foot and arm positions must be geared towards maintaining a square, and not an angular position, for transmitting power and generating push by straightening the legs. In the 3–4–1 scrummage, which came from South Africa, the contribution of the flankers is as significant as the locks. The tendency had been to go for the big flankers and a lighter more mobile No. 8 in the Tommy Bedford mould. The flankers traditionally have pincered on the scrum-half, and the No. 8 has been responsible for shepherding the outside-half.

Even though Louw was the quick breakaway and Stofberg the natural blind side type of flanker in the British game, the inflexible South Africans would retain the left and right system instead of open and blind. The Lions had adopted the same system, although Murphy, a typical Irish tearaway, would have preferred the presence of an open side flanker. The physical presence of Quinnell in the lineout would be crucial. At No. 5 between Colclough the middle jumper, and Squire at No. 6, he could lend the kind of protection that would ensure some return. O'Driscoll therefore at the lineout would have to play the open side flanker rule and concentrate on getting quickly to Naas Botha's boot.

The Springboks were slight favourites to win, the weather being fine and dry after a fortnight's rain. Still one felt that even money was about the right odds, and hoped that Tony Ward slept better than Naas Botha.

11
The First
Test

If Tony Ward and Naas Botha had taken one look at the Newlands pitch in Cape Town where the first Test was to be played, neither would have slept particularly well. The surface was a disgrace. The briefest shower of rain would have turned it into a swamp. It was a surface similar to the one upon which the Lions had launched their victory match six years previously. It was a great shame that a match of this importance should have to be played on a pitch of such poor quality. Excuses were made that the stands prevented the sun from getting at the areas along the touchlines which were bare and rutted, but the fact was that the pitch had been over-played with an average of three games a week since the start of the season. Over-riding financial considerations meant that the showpiece of the season was played on a surface which compared very unfavourably with other international venues around the world.

In one respect, however, the Springboks were a great deal more co-operative than they had been in the past. They allowed the public to watch their Thursday training session at Newlands. This was in contrast to 1974 when they went to the lengths of training behind prison doors. Not surprisingly, in view of its novelty value, hundreds turned up, and with most of them roaming all over the pitch the session was farcical. The backs attempted their moves in a cramped corner, the forwards scrummaged in another. The forwards attracted most interest, particularly from the visiting Press, because it soon became apparent that the scratch pack of Defence players brought in as opposition were causing acute embarrassment to their elders and presumably their betters. So much so that the loose-head prop, Piet Retieff, an heroic name in South African Rugby history, was banished to the touchline while the Springboks attempted to regain some of their confidence. Retieff was ignored after that, and he was very annoyed about it. At the end of the session the Springbok coach, Nellie Smith, complained bitterly about the interference by the crowd and threatened that in future they would revert to their secret sessions. It would have been far more sensible to have kept the crowd off the pitch.

The arrival the day before the match of the 'Cape Doctor' was the one medical presence the afflicted Lions could have done without. The 'Doctor' is a brisk south-east wind, so called because it drives the smoke and smog away from Cape Town. It also signals dry weather. However, the greatest obstacle standing in the Lions' way was the slim fair-haired man from Northern Transvaal called Naas Botha, who at the age of twenty-two was already endangering every South African scoring record. In fifty-three first-class games he had scored 661 points, an average of 12.5 per match. In five games of the current season he had totalled seventy-two points, twenty-six of them in the two Tests against the Jaguars. Against him the Lions were to put up Tony Ward, whose scoring feats had caused such astonishment in Europe two seasons previously. That was until the arrival of Ollie Campbell. It was the strangest irony that it was almost a year to the day, since Campbell ousted Ward from the Ireland side in Australia, that Ward was replacing Campbell in South Africa.

Neither Ward nor Botha could be happy about the pitch. For Botha, who had played most of his Rugby on the hard even surface of Transvaal, the transition would be more severe. After all the previews, Noel Murphy, who had enough experience of Rugby at this level to know what he was talking about, thought it would be close, and that the side making fewer mistakes would carry the day. He was right enough, but it was the Lions who made the mistakes, and the Springboks who won the match. It was also the Lions' misfortune that some mistakes had been made about which they could do nothing. One of these was the non-availability of a counter-attacking fullback.

Without such a man the Lions were unable to make use of the best loose possession of the day, and Naas Botha was free to boot the ball at will to any part of the field. It mattered not one whit that it often went straight to O'Donnell, the Lions' fullback, because there was nothing he could do about it except bang it back to touch.

It was difficult to believe that the Lions had won the scrums, won the loose ball, exceeded all expectations in the lineout, and yet lost the match, and what is more they lost by five tries to one. Ward was both hero and villain. His eighteen points broke the previous record held by Tom Kiernan, also of Ireland, for a Lion in a Test against South Africa, but Ward played no small part in two of the Springboks' tries.

The first was when his loose kick out of defence was taken by Gysie Pienaar, the Springboks' fullback, who immediately counter-attacked, kicking over Slemen's head. The ball bounced up very fortunately for him, and then he cut inside Ward, and Louw, who was supporting him, drove past various Lions, and got over the line as Carleton, O'Donnell, and Slemen tried to hold him up.

Again in the second half Ward's angled kick from behind a lineout was too far infield, and Germishuys started a counter-attack just outside his own 22. He passed to Pienaar, then the ball went to Mordt, and to Louw, who passed inside to Pienaar, and again out on the right touchline an overhead pass was taken magnificently by Germishuys with only a bit of an adjustment, and then he beat Richards and Slemen to finish with a score, a move that had begun at the other end.

Still the Lions had cause enough to be thankful for Ward's presence, particularly so because he was suffering from a bad bruise and ought not to have been on the field in the first place. On the day he outshone the much-praised Botha.

The Lions' forwards could have been excused if they had just given up and left the backs to stew in their own juice. Before half-time the backs had given away three tries, the first to Louw, the second to Willie du Plessis, when O'Donnell allowed the ball to bounce in front of him and du Plessis raced through unhampered to score between the posts, and the third when the ball popped up off O'Donnell's foot to van Heerden, who drove through some brittle tackling.

Botha kicked two conversions, but with three magnificent penalty goals by Ward for the Lions the Springboks were not quite out of sight at half-time. The Lions' forwards could hardly have given more. They had been in trouble in the scrums, in the lineout Beaumont and Colclough had put up stout resistance against van Heerden and Moolman, and in the loose, although trailing in the wake of Louw, Squire, O'Driscoll, and Quinnell had somehow managed to work back a fair supply of the ball. In the matter of support play, however, they were noticeably absent, and on the rare occasions when the ball got past the centres, neither Slemen nor Carleton could be assured of instant aid. It was lack of support perhaps which led to Carleton having to leave the field suffering from a rib injury. He was replaced by Ray Gravell.

If anything the forwards stepped up their efforts after half-time, and set about the task of chipping away at the Springboks' lead. First Ward kicked his fourth penalty goal, then at a lineout six metres from the Springbok line Kahts's throw to Moolman was not cleanly taken, the Lions got possession and Price was driven by a wedge over the line to make the score 16–16. By then the Springboks were beginning to show signs of wear and tear up front. Ward, with quite remarkable agility, took an indifferent pass from Patterson, jinked inside Louw, and although hopelessly off balance, chipped a left-footed dropped goal. The Lions looked safe; all they needed was control. Unfortunately for them the moment the ball left the forwards' cocoon, control was out of the question. Germishuys scored his try, which Botha converted, and the Lions were behind again.

If the forwards by then were close to despair they did not show it. Again they set about repairing the damage. They won a scrum, Quinnell held the ball, and Serfontein was caught off-side. Ward kicked his fifth penalty, this time from forty-five metres. Maybe there were some who could remember the first Test in 1955 when the Lions won 23–22 in Johannesburg because

Jack van der Schyff missed a conversion right at the end! It was a different tale this time.

It was a minute and a quarter into injury time when the winning score was made by South Africa. They threw into a lineout on the Lions' ten metre line, and when the ball reached David Smith in the centre Mordt, the strong-running Zimbabwe wing, came into the line, and passed to Willie du Plessis. Germishuys was next, then Mordt again. He was tackled by Patterson about four metres from the Lions' line. The ball was driven on by Willie du Plessis and Morne du Plessis, plus the pack. The Lions' pack joined in the action, holding up the Springboks, but Louw broke off and passed the ball on the Lions' line to Serfontein, who flopped over for the winning score.

There had to be a limit to the Lions' resilience. The final whistle went soon afterwards and the Springboks had beaten the Lions for the first time since 1968. The match was perhaps best summed up in those dying seconds when the Tourists' forwards, showing commendable loyalty to those who had done so little to deserve it, let the ball out to the backs. Down the line it went to David Richards, supposedly one of the most talented runners in the party. Instead of having a go at the defence he kicked harmlessly for the touchline, the ball rolled into touch, the final whistle sounded, and the Lions had lost. It was a match they could have won if their backs had shown even half the spirit of the forwards.

'I could not believe it'
by Carwyn James

In Auckland, New Zealand, at Eden Park in July 1977, I remember closing my eyes and reflecting during the course of the second half that what I was watching was about as probable as seeing snow on the same ground at Christmas. The Lions were giving one hell of a hammering to the All Blacks pack, and the New Zealand backs were giving Phil Bennett's boys a lesson in the art of back play. I could not believe it. Neither could I believe my eyes at Newlands. It was the same story of the Lions' supremacy up front, and the 'Boks behind the scrum playing Lions' Rugby. It is an inescapable fact that British back play has deteriorated considerably since the early seventies, and the forward play has improved to the same extent. While a team has forward supremacy and is winning quality possession, it is difficult not to be optimistic about its chances.

It took the Lions a fair while to settle down, probably because of the tension and anxiety to do well. In those circumstances the presence of experienced relaxed players is invaluable. Confrontations there had to be. At Potchefstroom van Heerden grabbed Quinnell by the throat, and when the Lion snarled the 'Bok' let go. At Newlands Morne du Plessis was a sitting target for an uncharacteristic punch thrown by Quinnell, and for the rest of the game, probably for a week, the Springbok captain sported a colourful 'China'. The Afrikaans writers were quick to point out that that punch to their popular skipper did more to motivate mighty deeds from the pack than any word spoken in the dressing room. Certainly the Springboks gave as good as they got in the early exchanges.

It was in the second half that the Lions gave them a lesson in the art of mauling and rucking, of winning and maintaining possession, of driving and rolling from one loose scrum to another, and hiding the ball from their opponents. It was superb controlled disciplined work from a well-drilled outfit, marred only by moments of indecision by Lions in key positions.

Fortunately this supremacy put the Lions in the right part of the field to kick goals, a department in which Tony Ward had impeccable qualifications, and despite the discomfort of his injury, he kicked well. So the Lions forwards never lost spirit even though they often lost ground because of the inefficiency of their backs. Patterson, as usual, was more than competent. Ward lacked vision, and not only did he kick indiscreetly out of hand, but he often set up the opposition in such admirable positions that even the Springboks felt they could counter and run at the opposition. That Pienaar, like the South African fullback Buchler at Cardiff in 1951, was made to look a world-beater speaks for itself. While Pienaar was enjoying one of the best afternoons of his Rugby career, his opposite number, O'Donnell, had one of his worst. It was a horrible baptism for him in Test Rugby. He caught the ball well enough, he showed all the courage in the world, but the poor lad was so hesitant when he had the ball in his hands that he looked completely lost, and kicked it aimlessly away hoping that something fruitful would happen. All the fruits went the way of the opposition, who were again set up for all kinds of counter-attacking play. O'Donnell too was often caught in two minds whether to go for the ball or to let it bounce.

Another unnecessary fault in the Lions' organization was in mid-field defensive alignment. The three midfield players must work in complete harmony, otherwise gaps will appear, and in this game they did to the extent that the defence looked fragmented and fragile. Carleton and Slemen were safe enough on the wings, but they were never given opportunities to run at the opposition. Still they stuck to their tasks like men, and Gravell did likewise when Carleton was injured.

Five tries to one is a hiding, and the fact that the Lions had a sufficient number of points to draw, or even to win, right up to the final whistle is a condemnation of the scoring in Rugby Football. The All Blacks won by six penalty goals to four tries by the Lions in 1959, and at Twickenham in 1980 England beat Wales by three penalty goals to two tries, and went on to win the championship. Members of the laws committee of the International Board were at Newlands, and I sincerely hope they made a mental note that in this running handling game matches can be won too often by the presence of a mighty kicker.

Having said that, two names spring immediately to mind: Francis Palmade, the French referee, and Naas Botha, the Springbok outside-half. At long last a major Test series was entrusted to neutral referees, and on the evidence of this first Test I think the experiment was an unqualified success. The onus on Palmade was heavy. The eyes of the Rugby world were upon him, and members of the sub-committee of the International Board were watching him. Palmade, at 41 years of age, is an experienced referee. He lives at Limoges, and he played most of his Rugby at Perpignon, first as a flanker and then at prop. He has twenty years of refereeing experience, including thirty internationals. He is an extremely fit man, and runs a minimum of eighty kilometres every week. He believes the referee should be conversant with the evolving tactics of the game as well as an authority on the laws.

M. Palmade had no difficulty in keeping up with the play; in fact he got in Patterson's way when Louw scored the first try of the series. Patterson bowled Palmade right over but failed to cut off Louw. Palmade was lucky that the try of momentum was not a controversial one because he had only a worm's eye view of it. Having watched a pretty abysmal display of refereeing by South Africa's No. 2 referee, Palmade was determined to show that he was the master of ceremonies, and that he was fully conversant with the definition which maintains that the price of discipline is eternal vigilance. In fact it was a scrupulously clean game. The players had respect for the referee, and they got on with the game. His refereeing of the lineouts was first-class. He was completely aware too of the intricacies of front row play, and he never allowed the game to deteriorate to the low standards that had been set in the game at Stellenbosch the previous week. He allowed play to develop in the mauls and rucks when he felt that there was a chance of the ball emerging.

A referee can usually be judged by the proximity of the whistle to his mouth as he runs about the field. M. Palmade's whistle was sufficiently far away to allow him time to play the advantage, and the advantage law is the most important one in the book. A referee should not be judged on the number of penalties he gives to one side or the other, or how many penalties can be kicked at goal. Such judgement suggests honesty or dishonesty and such a yardstick should not be applied to a neutral referee. M. Palmade was far more honest than his critics. We did not see a better South African referee.

Still the Springboks were not happy with his performance,

and 'Butch' Lochner asked for a meeting with him and the Lions. Millar declined, saying the Lions were satisfied with M. Palmade's interpretations, and the meeting never took place because the International Board, who had arrived by that time as guests of the South African Board, stopped it, saying that it was against the spirit of the game.

During the first half of the game there was only one attempted goal kick by Botha, which he fluffed. In fact he did not have too happy a day with his kicking. Perhaps the indifferent turf on a ground at sea level did not help him, but some of his line kicking gave a loud and clear warning that on the High Veldt he would be a threat to the Lions.

Although pride had been restored by a magnificent effort of the Lions' forwards and the boot of Ward, the figures five and one kept recurring like a bad dream. Yet the optimist had to say that such forward effort as this by the Lions if repeated, must produce victory.

At the after-match function, Danie Craven expressed his obvious delight, saying it was one of the proudest moments of his life. He also criticized the British Press for remarks made after the Stellenbosch game. One journalist had described the five white forwards who played that day as 'yobos', a singularly unfortunate word which received far more attention than it deserved. It was certainly not accurate. Hennie Becker, one of the forwards, is among the least combative of the Springbok locks, and de Villiers Visser, at the age of twenty-one, was hardly likely to 'mix it' with an international team. Anyhow Craven went on to say that South Africa had done everything possible to bring about integration in sport, and they were damned if they were going to be criticized by a bunch of touring Pressmen.

'Why don't you stop interfering, and leave us to our own devices?' he asked. One might have replied that if South Africans had been left to their own devices, the Lions would not have been there. It was an ill-timed and ill-advised speech and lost Dr Craven and South Africa several friends. One journalist wrote to him saying he would not attend any more after-match functions given by the South African Board because he had turned against his paper's policy in favour of the tour, and was a most disappointed and disillusioned man. Afterwards on the telephone Dr Craven tried to placate him, but a great deal of damage had been done.

So much so that one wondered whether it was not time that Dr Craven stepped down gracefully from his position as President of the South African Rugby Board, a position he has occupied for twenty-five years.

It was left to Syd Millar, with an amusing speech, to take the heat out of the situation. He thanked 'Lord Stellenbosch' for his remarks, thanked the Springboks for the game, thanked his own boys for their efforts, and à propos nothing at all, reflected upon the Lions' stay in Orange Free State, where there were no oranges, nothing was free, and everything was in a hell of a state. Millar made excellent speeches throughout the tour, and Bill Beaumont, as captain, always spoke naturally and well.

12
The Lions Go Shooting

That night after the first Test it was with almost indecent haste that the management began to make arrangements for Andy Irvine to join the party. The position was certainly desperate enough. Neither Hay nor O'Donnell was able to provide what the Lions needed most – a player who could turn defence into attack. Carleton's injury had been diagnosed as a sprung rib cartilage, and Elgan Rees was still in Johannesburg receiving treatment for a knee ligament injury, so the Lions had only one specialist wing, Mike Slemen. Although it was not generally known at the time, his stay in South Africa was to be dramatically cut short. His wife who was six months pregnant was having a difficult time, and to make matters worse she had caught a virus from their young son, and was in hospital. Naturally she was depressed and finding things difficult to cope with. It was only because of Noel Murphy's powers of persuasion that Slemen went on to the field at all at Newlands. It was clear his place was at home with his wife and family, so the Lions had to prepare themselves for the worst.

Slemen's loss was the biggest blow they had suffered so far. He was the one back who had played consistently to form; if anything better than he had played in the domestic season. He had scored five tries in as many matches, and there were plenty more for him on the hard grounds of the Transvaal. His defensive qualities were of inestimable value.

The Sunday after the Test was a day when the team found ways of seeking solace. Some took advantage of the glorious weather to go up Table Mountain, others remained in the hotel to let alcohol take the strain. By Monday the worst was over;

here was another town, another match, for which to prepare. The town was Windhoek in South West Africa, an area rich in semi-precious stones and game. So on the Tuesday a shoot was organized. The Lions were represented by 'Colonel' Murphy, 'Captain' Beaumont, and 'Corporals' Gravell and Tomes. The war zone covered about 25,000 acres owned by a local farmer, and the weapon was a .300 magnum rifle. Kudu, a species of antelope, were the target.

Murphy was the first to blaze away from the roof of the truck, but such was the kick-back that there was a great deal more danger to Murphy than there was to any game, and he all but toppled off his perch. The next was Gravell, who with perfect aim got down a female kudu – 'Wales 3, Army 1, IRA nil', shouted Gravell in triumph. Murphy, who had by then missed again twice, was not amused, and with each round costing about £2, neither was the farmer. The best was saved quite rightly for skipper Beaumont who scored a direct hit on a superb bull, the horns of which were to be mounted and sent back to the Fylde Rugby Club.

It had been a great day, voted one of the best of the tour by all save Murphy who was heard to mutter on the homeward journey, 'The only things I kill are Lions on a Monday morning'.

The idea that anything was going to be easy for the Lions on this trip was by then so preposterous that it was not worth considering, but for an international side the match against the South African Country XV, it was hoped, would provide some light relief following the heart-breaking events at the weekend. The local XV was made up of players who took part in a Sport Pienaar competition – one for teams not participating in the Currie Cup. At that time South West Africa were the holders of the trophy, but like all midweek sides had made attempts to bolster their strength. Hennie Shields, the Cape Coloured centre, would be making his third appearance against the Lions in as many weeks, and acquaintance would also be renewed with Morgan Cushe, who captained the SARA XV at East London, and Solomon Mhlaba, the fullback that day. All three had toured Britain with the Barbarians. The rest of the team would comprise

white players, some of whom had been given leave from opera
tions against SWAPO on the border 500 miles to the north. A
least they would be fit and hard.

With no genuine wings in the party the Lions had to improvise
so Woodward played on the right and Morgan on the left
Woodward had certain qualifications to be classed with Morgar
as a utility back in the party. He had played outside-half for
England Schools, he had also turned out at fullback, but he hac
never before played on the wing. In view of the instability ir
midfield it was perhaps time to consider Morgan as a centre. He
was fast off the mark, possessed a fine pair of hands, and hi:
defence was secure. It could have been that many of the midfield
problems had stemmed from bad distribution from outside-half.
so to get the best from this re-arranged threequarter line a lot
depended on Gareth Davies, who was making his first appearance after injuring his shoulder in the opening match.

Apart from weaknesses in the backs the Lions had also to
inject, somehow or other, more pace into their loose forward
play before the second Test. Both flankers, Gareth Williams and
Colm Tucker, had the opportunity to press their claims. The
decision to give Bruce Hay the captaincy was more of a
psychological boost for the Scot than anything else. It was two
weeks since he had had a game, and with Andy Irvine about to
join the party he might find himself short of opportunities to
convince the selectors that he had more to offer than was
apparent in his first two matches.

The Lions had to be thankful for small mercies, and there
were some things to be thankful for in their 27–7 win over the
South African Country XV, The most important thing in the
light of all that had gone before, was that they survived the
match without further injury. Davies played with an authority
that was markedly absent in the first Test, and his half-back
partner, John Robbie, was the outstanding performer of the
day. He sent out a stream of fast accurate passes, the very variety
of which was obviously to the liking of Davies. That was as far
as the good news went. The bad made longer reading.

The tackling was at times non-existent, loose forward play

was pedestrian, the handling was careless, and there was an obession with complicated midfield ploys when it would have been far more productive to do the simple thing. The use of Gravell as a battering ram was time and energy mis-spent. Not only did it fail to gain ground, but it disrupted a backline that looked easily capable of out-running the opposition. Renwick improved on his Saturday performance, but not much, and on the wings Woodward and Morgan were full of running, although Morgan was inclined to carry the ball too far before looking for support. Of course his problem was that again the support was seldom there. This was a major worry for the selectors. They simply had no one within shouting distance of Louw, who had inflicted so much damage at Newlands. At fullback Hay played with a lot more confidence than he had done, but was not very comfortable chasing the ball across field. He fielded courageously, and on several occasions made some telling incursions into the threequarter line, which might have led to greater things had the support play been of reasonable quality.

The Lions, with a strong wind in front of them, managed to score sixteen points in the first half, with two penalty goals by Davies, and tries by Beattie and Renwick. Beattie's try, which Davies converted, was the result of the best scrummage shove of the day, the Lions driving their opponents back from a five-metre scrum and Beattie making the touchdown. Renwick owed his try to Orr, the pick of the forwards, and a real threat to Clive Williams for a Test place. Orr peeled from the lineout, drove into midfield, fed Robbie, and a quick pass from Gravell gave Renwick space. Renwick, with Woodward unmarked outside him, dummied, got away with it, and scored, much to his own huge relief no doubt. Had he failed Woodward might have felt moved to make some comment. Tobias kicked a penalty goal for the Country XV, so the Lions led 16–3 at half-time.

They could have had a rewarding second half. That they scored only eleven more points was mainly due to their own incompetence, although some credit must be given to the opposition defence, and some blame to a referee who had little idea of the off-side law. Twice he incurred the wrath of Wheeler, the Lions' hooker, who was seen to push his elbow into the referee and was lucky to get away with it. It was understandable that the Lions were frustrated by some of the decisions, but it did little good to argue, and was merely evidence of indiscipline in the team at the time.

The Lions scored two more tries, one by Woodward after the best combined move of the match, and the other by Gareth Williams who was on hand to support Hay's charge. Davies kicked a third penalty goal, and Charles Williams scored the sole try for the Country XV. The Lions' problems continued.

Carwyn James viewed the incident between Wheeler and the referee as follows:

The match was punctuated by too much bad whistle from a poor referee. When Wheeler was desperately trying to cover the extra ten metres awarded against the Lions for questioning the award of a penalty, he accidentally nudged the referee, who, probably because Wheeler had queried some of his strange decisions, thought it was intentional. When we arrived in Johannesburg the following day a member of the International Board asked me for an explanation of the incident, which by that time I had almost forgotten. A prominent member of the South African Board had been in touch with him on the telephone. Obviously the referee had been in touch with Dr Craven.

The Lions in successive midweek matches had suffered two poor referees, and both games had been staccato, unspectacular, and lacking in any sort of rhythm. The Country XV included four of the best Leopards, and another, Charlie Williams the try-scorer, came on as a substitute. Solomon Mhlaba had a most uncertain game, Shields looked nowhere near international class, Cushe was his usual honest self, and Errol Tobias showed some flair, but his linking was indifferent. The convenor of the Springbok selectors, 'Butch' Lochner, had predicted early in the year that probably this season would see a black player in a

Springbok jersey. After this match one thought that his prediction would most likely be wrong.

For the Lions the performance of Robbie was the most pleasing feature. In his quickness of delivery, and his reading of the match, he showed that he was capable of giving performances of Test standard. Davies, playing well within himself, rode a smother-tackle from behind and came through a difficult match unharmed, and obviously fit for the Transvaal game and the second Test. Although both Gravell and Renwick are one hundred percenters they failed to find the fluency which stretches the opposition. Woodward, an elusive runner, looked at ease on the right wing, and Morgan played his best game of the tour so far. Hay was full of enthusiasm and courage, and looked a much better player than he had done in any previous match, but he still had not the legs to turn defence into attack, and if the Irvine and Hay alliance was to be a serious consideration for the next Test then Irvine had to be at fullback.

The pack played well enough, but I wished that Gareth Williams had been on the open side and Colm Tucker on the blind. The Lions ought to have scored half a century of points against the rather weak opposition.

13
Irvine Raises Hopes

The events of the week following the Windhoek match, we felt, would almost certainly determine the success or failure of the tour. Having lost the first Test, the Lions would have to do what no other touring side in history had achieved, namely to win the last three Tests of the four-match series. So the selection of the side for the match against Transvaal at the Wanderers' ground in Johannesburg was of immense significance. Few would quibble with the selection of all eight forwards who had played at Newlands. Barring accidents all eight would play again in the second Test at Bloemfontein.

The backs presented the problems, and in view of the difficulties at fullback it was no surprise to find Andy Irvine pitched into the side despite having spent most of the last month nursing a hamstring injury. Irvine is without equal as a runner from defensive positions, while his ability to inject pace into a cumbersome looking back line would give the Lions greater width in attack. The selection of Bruce Hay on the left wing, a position he occupied for Scotland, meant that he could perform the functions of auxiliary fullback when Irvine was occupied with attacking duties, and he would support Irvine under the high ball. One of the points of selecting a counter-attacking fullback was that he would be flanked by wings who could run equally well out of defence.

However the signs were clear that the Lions had resigned themselves to playing a game that involved mainly the forwards and the half-backs. In Gareth Davies they had the right outside-half for the job. It had been his tactical kicking at Twickenham earlier in the year that had kept the Ringer-less Welshmen in the game, and at Windhoek he had demonstrated the value of thoughtful kicking. It would be the first time on tour that he had played with Colin Patterson as his scrum-half, and that was a measure of how great the injury problems had been. It would be the eighth half-back partnership in nine games.

Transvaal had one of the biggest packs in the country. Four of them had Test experience. It would have been five, but Moaner van Heerden withdrew on the morning of the match with an ankle injury, and that was to keep him out of the Springbok Test side. The four Test men were Richard Prentis the loose head prop, Johann Strauss, the tight head, Kevin de Klerk in the second row who had played against the Jaguars, and Donald MacDonald, the No. 8 who had won seven caps for Scotland, the last of them against England two years previously. Behind the scrum Transvaal were not so well equipped, although they had Gerry Germishuys on the left, a try-scorer at Newlands. Their record in the Currie Cup was more an encouragement to the Lions than to themselves, but the Lions knew by then they must disregard any form guides.

The match had to be played at the Wanderers' ground because the more famous venue in Johannesburg, Ellis Park, was being rebuilt. It was no coincidence that the introduction of two players of the calibre of Irvine and Davies into the back division produced easily the most convincing performance of the tour. The Lions' 32–12 victory over Transvaal was, if anything, flattering to the home side. Just when it seemed the Lions' fortunes were improving, however, fate dealt them the cruellest blow. Irvine, whose pace had given them a variety of attacking options previously denied them, suffered a recurrence of the hamstring injury which had forced him to withdraw from the party five weeks previously.

The delight in victory was soured not only by Irvine's mishap, but by the fact that David Richards dislocated his shoulder, and could take no further part in the tour. At a conservative estimate it would be four weeks until he could play again, which meant that the Lions were seeking a seventh replacement. The man they had asked for was the England and Leicester centre, Paul Dodge.

The sadness for Richards was that he, in common with the rest of the backs, was beginning to show something like his true form. Ray Gravell was another, and Bruce Hay, strangely for one who plays most of his Rugby at fullback, looked a great deal happier on the wing. His commitment had never been in doubt, and that day against Transvaal he played with a determination that carried him into the Test side.

The Lions' forwards continued where they had left off at Newlands. They were superior in the scrums, the rucks, and mauls, but at a disadvantage in the loose where their lack of pace was again evident, and in the lineout where de Klerk at No. 2 took enough clean catches to win Test selection in place of van Heerden.

The principal difference between the Lions' display against Transvaal and the one the week previously at Newlands lay in the fact that Davies was able to put the possession gained to the best possible use. His tactical kicking was reminiscent of Barry John at his best, and the break he made which led to Clive Woodward's second try also had the look of John about it. All this came from a man who had played only two full games since leaving the field in the Wales v Scotland match three months before. He set up three of the Lions' six tries, the most that they had scored in one match; he was completely at ease with his partner, Patterson, who if anything improved on John Robbie's midweek display at Windhoek. Patterson in fact scored the best try with a lightning scamper after John O'Driscoll and Phil Orr had done the donkey work.

Orr, who had a tough opponent in Strauss, came through his ordeal extremely well. Woodward left no one in doubt about his class on the wing. His elegant running was a joy, and coming as it did against the Springbok wing Germishuys, was a psychological boost before the second Test.

Irvine, who hit a post each time with three kicks at goal, eventually succeeded with a penalty from fifty metres, but it was his contribution in the broken play which was so heartening for the Lions, and he made at least two superb tackles. Davies made three of the tries, first by switching play and giving

Woodward a try, the second by kicking high so that Richards could chase in when there was indecision in the Transvaal defence, and the third he scored himself beating Peter Wilkinson and Jurie Fourie to the touchdown. Graham Price also got a try, Woodward, in addition to his two tries, kicked a penalty goal and a conversion. Transvaal's try was scored by Maritz, and converted by Lee Barnard who also kicked two penalties.

Carwyn James noted after this game:

While Naas Botha's boot was battering Western Province at Newlands in a repetition of the previous season's Currie Cup final to the tune of 14 points, including another hat-trick of dropped goals, the Lions were bewildering Transvaal with their drill in loose scrums.

The fact is that the Lions were as good as they had been in the Test, and Transvaal's huge pack had no answer to their driving and their rolling.

Both as game-keepers and poachers Bill Beaumont's forwards were much superior, and at long last there were two backs capable of using quality possession. It was only at the front of the lineout that the Lions had a problem in dealing with the well protected de Klerk. In the scrum the bulky Strauss was back at his old tricks of collapsing the scrummage. The referee was far too lenient with him. Orr, a substitute for Clive Williams who was suffering from a stomach upset, was patient with Strauss, and he played a lively game in the loose. Davies and Patterson played beautifully at half-back. Patterson got the ball away with the speed of a bullet to the cool composed Davies who was the personification of nonchalance. He certainly had the presence of Barry John. Davies's temperament was never in doubt. He missed a sitter of a penalty in the first few minutes, cheekily tried to drop a goal, missed that too, and then settled down to create tries. It was a masterly performance which brought the best out of Richards. It was so tragic that Richards dislocated his shoulder at a time when the Lions really needed him. Gravell liaised well with Richards and Davies, and he too gave his best performance so far. He had been promising an outside break for some time, and at last he achieved the almost impossible

Over-enthusiasm to tackle caused the heart-beat to stumble occasionally when the outside centre over-ran his colleague and created the half-gap, but while overall the alignment was by no means perfect in loose ball situations, it was better. Hay played with his heart on the left-wing, tackling fiercely, and only once did his opposite number beat him for pace. However, once might be too often in a Test match. Woodward was quite brilliant. His dancing, jinking approach graced the green pastures of the Wanderers' ground. His place-kicking was more positive than that of the 'professionals' and both his tries were memorable.

Irvine's mere presence was enough. He played with the panache of the experienced campaigner which must have given confidence to the other fourteen. It was by far the Lions' best performance.

14
Zimbabwe Says 'No'

Originally the Lions' itinerary included a match against Zimbabwe in Salisbury. It had long been the custom to play a match there when the country was called Rhodesia. Quite early in the tour, though, the Zimbabwe Government said they considered the match inappropriate and an embarrassment to their country, and advised the Zimbabwe Rugby Union to call it off. They said they welcomed teams from abroad, but not teams who treated them as part of South Africa, and that was what the Lions were doing on this tour. The Zimbabwe Rugby Union had a meeting with the Minister of Sport, a Mrs Teurai Rhopa Nhongo, a lady who is twenty-five years old, and whose first two names mean 'Spilled Blood'. Barely six months before she had been a freedom fighter. She took the matter to the Prime Minister, and it was obvious that although sporting relations between South Africa and Zimbabwe were continuing almost as normal, there was little chance of the match being played. Currie Cup matches could be played, but the Lions' visit was another matter. Perhaps if the Lions had agreed to play a couple of games in Zimbabwe, one of them a full international, it might have been all right, but as part of the tour of South Africa it was not on. So Mr Mugabe ruled it out, saying that he had an obligation to take a joint stand with other nations against apartheid.

Instead of the Lions' match, Zimbabwe played Public Schools Wanderers, who included Fergus Slattery and several players who would have graced the proceedings south of the border. The injury jinx extended to Salisbury, though, for it was in training for that game that Peter Squires, whom the Lions selectors had passed over, but who would have been in demand as a replacement, dislocated his elbow. His replacement, Alan Morley, another former England wing, scored all five of the Wanderers tries in their 39–20 victory, and Les Cusworth, the Leicester outside-half, scored nineteen points.

The Zimbabwe Government's attitude was pointedly expressed by Mrs Nhongo, who attended the curtain raiser between the Zimbabwe'n Under-25s and the Zambia Under-25s, and walked out of the ground with her Deputy Minister before the Wanderers appeared on the pitch. Twelve thousand people watched the match. Perhaps their feelings were best expressed by the lone voice which cried, 'Come on Rhodesia, you're playing like a bunch of Zimbabwe'ns!'

The replacement fixture for the Lions was against Eastern Transvaal at Springs. The Rugby ground there is one of the least attractive in South Africa. Springs is an industrial town some thirty miles east of Johannesburg, and the ground, set amid industrial buildings, is almost bare except for some frosted brown grass. It is forbidding and depressing, and twelve years earlier the Lions prop, John O'Shea from Cardiff, had been sent off there.

However, before going into this area of gloom the Lions had some fun. By the Sunday evening after their fine victory over Transvaal, the other 'Test series' stood at one-all. The Lions, augmented by some guests, had beaten the Springboks by five wickets with five overs remaining. Billy Beaumont led the side which included Peter Wheeler, Clive Woodward, John Robbie, Ollie Campbell, and Jeff Squire, while the most distinguished guest was none other than Graeme Pollock, who in happier days had entertained the British cricket public. One could not help realizing that his seventy-nine runs probably had a lot to do with the Lions' success. While Wheeler had the greatest difficulty in making himself comfortable behind the wicket because his borrowed flannels were a couple of sizes too small, Chris Lander of the *Daily Mirror* returned career-best figures of two for thirty-one off one over. The fielding was of a very high standard. Robbie stopped everything that came near him, although he estimated that some of it must have been travelling at about two hundred miles per hour.

Even in play, though, the Lions suffered their customary injury . On his way to lunch Robbie turned his ankle on a water hydrant. At the time it seemed to be a minor twinge, but it was to have important repercussions. Incidentally the Lions played this game of cricket for charity, to benefit the black community. The proceeds were given to the Ezibeleni Orthopaedic Home for Crippled Black Children.

For John Carleton, Terry Holmes, and Campbell, the Eastern Transvaal match was a make-or-break occasion. Carleton insisted on playing. 'If I can't play I might as well leave and make way for someone who can', he said. It seemed unlikely, though, that he would get through the match without further damage to his ribs. However he was adamant, and the management indulged him. For Holmes it would be his first match since dislocating his shoulder two weeks previously, and his partner, Campbell, would be making only his second appearance of the tour. If the Lions' bad luck continued there was little chance that all three would survive the game intact. In fact they did not. Holmes twisted his knee ligaments in the first few minutes and had to leave the field midway through the first half.

Still, at the beginning of the week the Lions were in better spirits, greatly encouraged by the news that Andy Irvine's hamstring strain might be no more than the reaction to his first full game for two months. Irvine missed the training session and went instead to the physiotherapist, and came back much happier. He could take no risks, though, and after a light training spin went back for more physiotherapy.

John Beattie was down to play at No. 8, but he had to retire to bed with a touch of influenza. He was keen to play, though, because after such a promising start he seemed to have lost his edge, and he needed to regain his appetite for the game, and become more involved in the close quarter work. It was a disappointment that he had not improved as much as most of us thought he would. His speed was a great asset to the back row, but his play did not quite reach the desired standard.

The appearance of Bruce Hay for the second successive match on the left wing confirmed the selectors' intention to play him there in the second Test. He had worked hard all along and it looked as if his efforts were not going to be in vain. Hay is a most whole-hearted player, and that is a great consideration for a Test.

Eastern Transvaal were not in the top thirteen South African provincial sides. They played in the Sport Pienaar competition, the league for sides who do not play in the Currie Cup. Neither were they quite the force they had been in 1968 when John O'Shea had been sent off, but they would give the Lions a reasonable test. Altogether the Springs ground seemed an unhappy one, for during the match between Eastern Transvaal and North West Cape the Saturday before the Lions' game, the Eastern Transvaal flanker Kleinboet Fourie had been ordered to the 'sinbin' for over-zealous play. Despite that – the 'sinbin' means only a temporary absence – Eastern Transvaal won by 55–4, scoring nine tries. At least they, unlike many of the midweek sides, had not been strengthened by the inclusion of several guest players. They were a bona fide combination.

Within five minutes of the kick-off it became very clear why O'Shea had been sent off in that match twelve years before. Eastern Transvaal always had the reputation of playing a spoiling game, which was frustrating to those who wanted to enjoy their Rugby. To play like that for eighty minutes, however, required some assistance from the referee. On this occasion Eastern Transvaal had a most enthusiastic referee in Mr Stoney Steenkamp, a schoolmaster who seemed to have done little homework on interpreting the laws of the game. He was the least efficient referee the Lions had encountered so far, which probably qualified him for a place in the *Guinness Book of Records*. The penalty count against the Lions was in the ratio of three to one, which had the effect of disrupting whatever rhythm the Lions had shown earlier in the match. That was when Carleton, playing for his tour life, scored a try, and Campbell converted it. In fact the only good points to emerge from the game, from the Lions' point of view, were the confirmation of the fitness of both Carleton and Campbell. The latter kicked four penalty goals, a dropped goal, and a conversion, scoring a total of seventeen points. For Holmes, though, it was another blow in the unbelievable run of bad luck. His kneee ligaments were torn, and, along with David Richards and Fran Cotton, he would be returning home.

Bad though the refereeing was, it was impossible to ignore the fact that international touring teams should easily be able to overcome such frustrations. The Lions' midweek side seemed incapable of doing so, and were run uncomfortably close by an extremely poor local XV for whom the outside-half, Geere, kicked all the points with four penalty goals and a dropped goal.

Carwyn James had these thoughts on the game:

It was easily the worst game of the tour up to that point. It was sad because the Lions needed a relaxing sort of game, and they needed to score well over thirty points, which they had not done so far. We all wished we had gone to Zimbabwe, as one or two of the British journalists did, carrying Syd Millar's message to Peter Squires, to the effect that he should avoid getting injured. What with the doubt about Carleton being able to get through this particular game, and the fact that the selectors would not risk Elgan Rees, it was very much on the cards that Squires would have been called for. However, Squires was indeed injured and so the Lions' jinx had extended to Zimbabwe.

As for the game at Springs, Mr Steenkamp's refereeing was very one-sided, and I could not understand it, because he is a coach at one of the leading high schools in Bloemfontein. He is highly regarded as a coach, and although obviously he knows the game backwards, he never got into this one at all, and there was a lot of niggling and aggravation. It is often said that it takes two good sides to make good Rugby football; in this game we saw none at all.

Carleton's try came after five minutes. After that there were no more tries, and this was a midweek match! That just about sums it up.

I must say one or two things about Carleton. He gave up his job in order to go on this tour, and here he was playing in a great deal of pain. He has the greatest courage. He was so determined to prove to the Lions' management that he could get through the game, that he showed no signs at all of the pain he was suffering. After that display I thought he thoroughly deserved his place in the second Test, and I was delighted when he was chosen.

The other player who also came of age in this game at Springs was John Beattie. He revealed himself early in the tour as a young man who had the potential of being a very good back row forward, and one who could learn a great deal about the game on this tour. He would make a good No. 8, but he just did not have the aggression that is needed at the highest level. After the first two or three training sessions Beattie said he thought he had no chance in competition with Derek Quinnell. That is not the stuff from which Test players are made. No matter how good a player Quinnell was, there was always the chance he might be injured. It was up to Beattie to prove that he was a good number two. Up to this stage I thought he was not even that, because if Quinnell was not played in a Test then Jeff Squire would move from flanker to No. 8.

In this match however Beattie showed more aggression than he had in any other game, and his confrontation on many occasions with the opposition No. 5, who was a niggling sort of player, was something that I enjoyed. There was little enough to enjoy, but this display by Beattie must have been an encouraging sign for the management.

Still, one wanted to forget this day, because a good touring side should have been above niggling, and they ought to have scored far more tries than they did. They allowed themselves to be put under pressure unnecessarily. The tone of the match persisted even at the reception afterwards, when the mayor of the town made a speech which was far too long, and somewhat inconsequential. We were quite glad to leave Springs.

15
Bloemfontein Again

Bloemfontein is not the most pleasant town in South Africa. It has the highest pollution rate in the country, and unless you are a fanatical lover of old steam trains the only reason to go there is to play or watch Rugby Football. The train museum is famous and indeed quite wonderful for those who like that sort of thing. The Rugby ground is very fine too, although it certainly would not pass a safety scrutiny based on British standards. In fact we thought it was highly dangerous. Most of the scaffolding was erected in such a way that people could easily fall through it. Anyhow, that is where the second Test was to be played, and the Lions arrived in town the day after leaving the gloom of Springs. It was not of course their first visit, because they had beaten the Orange Free State there just over three weeks previously, so they were not too downcast by their surroundings, as they prepared for the match which they must win to keep the series alive.

Since their last-minute defeat in the first Test at Newlands a fortnight previously, the Lions had lost three more Test players, Mike Slemen, David Richards and Terry Holmes. Their morale was sustained, though, by the fine performance against Transvaal the previous Saturday, and they had had to live on that memory throughout that trying week. Although the game at Springs had little to commend it, the fact that the party was still in good spirits showed that on the whole they had the right temperament, and they were buoyed up too by the determination of John Carleton, which had been such a fine example. It was such determination as his that might help them level the series.

Five changes had been made in the Test team, all in the back division, and two of them, those of fullback and outside-half, being of the greatest tactical significance. Gareth Davies replaced Tony Ward at outside-half. Although Ward had almost kicked the Lions to victory at Newlands, in the end he kicked them to defeat. Davies, we hoped, would not be so charitable. He would partner Colin Patterson, to reform an alliance they had made six years previously for the Universities Athletic Union against the Public Schools Wanderers. No one watching that match could have foreseen that those two young men would come together again to challenge the Springboks in the most vital match of the tour. Alas, the night before the match Davies had a bad dream. He saw his left knee terribly swollen, and when he awoke in the middle of the night he could almost feel the pain. It was a premonition that came true. He had to limp off the field ten minutes from the end of the Test match, and another key Lion had finished his tour.

Happily Andy Irvine was none the worse for his hamstring strain the previous Saturday, and would play at fullback where we hoped his presence would be a deterrent to Naas Botha's kicking. The disturbing thought about Botha was that, like a great batsman, he must be expected to come off at some time in the series. He had failed at Newlands, but closer to his own patch he might very well succeed.

Ray Gravell and Clive Woodward formed a new centre partnership where David Richards and Jim Renwick had been in the first Test. Woodward's inclusion in the centre was surprising because he had been playing well on the right wing, and with his outside swerve that was probably his best position. However Carleton had had such a good game against Eastern Transvaal, and had shown such courage, that he was given the right wing position. The South African Press were giving Gravell more support than he had from the British Press, probably because they like a bulldozing type of centre with plenty of aggression much more than the British do. It is the same in New Zealand, where physical qualities are more highly regarded than pure skill. In any case it looked as if the Lions' management had decided not to use the width of the field but to use the crash ball in the middle and play back to the strength, which was the pack. This was a developing tactic during the tour, and so Gravell was being used more and more.

Bruce Hay was on the left wing in place of Slemen. He had come into favour not because of his skill or pace, but because of his one hundred per cent determination and ability to tackle. It was important to have a strong tackler opposite Ray Mordt, the strong-running wing from Zimbabwe. We felt there was a theme of defence rather than attack in the choice of the threequarter line. The pack that had done so well in the first Test was unchanged.

The Springboks had made only one change. Moaner Van Heerden still had the ankle injury which had prevented him from playing against the Lions for Transvaal. Almost as a punishment, we thought, because there did not appear to have been very much wrong with him and he had not shown great enthusiasm to get the ankle right, he had been replaced by his Transvaal team-mate Kevin de Klerk, who had played in the matches against the Jaguars. He had played very well in the lineouts against the Lions too.

The Springboks had said they would run the ball, and we thought that was more of a threat than a promise. The more we reflected on their five tries at Newlands, though, the more we realized that with all the opportunities that were presented to them, they could not help but run in tries. The Lions must not allow that freedom this time.

The Lions' pack was now a formidable unit, possibly as well drilled as the 1974 pack, although lacking the pace of Fergus Slattery and the phenomenal tackling of Mervyn Davies. The absence of pace in the back row had thrown an additional strain on the midfield defence and that was where the Lions had been vulnerable to counter-attack. Gravell, although he had improved in attack to the extent that he looked for spaces to run into rather than opponents, remained undisciplined in his defensive alignment, and David Smith, the Zimbabwe centre, had the speed to exploit this.

The Springboks had increased their overall weight advantage and had added to their strength in the lineout, but they had sacrificed their expertise in the rucks and mauls and their mobility in the loose. They were going to persevere with Theuns Stofberg on the flank – Tommy Bedford, that great former Springbok No. 8, former Oxford University captain and Richmond player, thought Stofberg should be on the blind side – and it turned out that they were right to do so. Stofberg scored a try. It was just the Lions' luck that Stofberg had a painful knee on the Thursday before the match but recovered in time to play.

Faux Pas

There was trouble in the newspapers on the morning of the second Test. 'Butch' Lochner, the convenor of the Springbok selectors, was quoted as saying that the Lions were cheating. Chris Swanepoel, a South African journalist, quoted Lochner in his paper *The Citizen*, which is the South African Government's paper, as saying 'I expect the Lions to continue with the subtle obstruction which spoiled most of the lineouts in the first Test, but this time we shall be able to counter it. The Springboks have proved to the world in three Test matches this year (two against South America) that they play their Rugby hard but clean; the Lions on the other hand do the opposite.' Swanepoel added that those who live by the sword should die by the sword.

It was reminiscent of Ivan Vidanovich's statement in 1971 when he was the All Blacks' coach. There had been a bloody battle in Canterbury in New Zealand, and before the second Test Vodanovich said that if the Lions killed the rucks as they had done in the first Test, they could expect something akin to Passchendaele. He was trying to put up a smoke screen to cover the Canterbury scene. The present situation was not as bad as that, but Lochner's statement sounded worse, coming as it did after Dr Craven's outburst against the British Press following the first Test. The Lions' camp was very upset, and after the second Test Syd Millar made his protest. He deplored Lochner's statement and the inference that the Lions were not playing within the laws of the game. He said it was an unjust attack on the Lions. 'Rugby Football is not a war', he said. 'We have only come here to play Rugby.'

That was his speech at the after-match function. Morne du Plessis, the Springbok captain, did what he could to smooth things over. He regretted very much any comments that had been made and might have been taken out of context or misquoted. He gave Lochner the benefit of the doubt by saying they might have been misquoted. If that were not so, he added, then the comments were very much to be regretted.

All through the tour du Plessis proved himself to be not only a exceptionally good leader but a very fine person. The Springbok captain is in a difficult position because he is placed between two extremes. On one side are those who think he is their champion for 'stuffing the Lions out of sight' and taking complete revenge for 1974 by winning at all costs; and on the other are those who think that because the Springbok captain has greater influence than almost any other person in the country he ought to make gestures of protest against the government's policies, for example by refusing to lead his team on to the field.

Du Plessis told us on another occasion that he was not a political animal. He knew all about the pressure on him to be so, but he hoped he had a sense of fairness, and that it came through in his everyday life as well as in his Rugby. He was desperately keen to win of course, but he considered the manner in which his team won was far more important.

Also he had a personal life to lead, and when he was not playing Rugby he wanted to get away from all the pressure that was on him as captain.

After Lochner's statement, Dr Craven had held a meeting with Lochner, Millar and Swanepoel in which he tried to smooth things over. Afterwards he announced that neither Nellie Smith, the manager, nor Lochner was to make statements to the Press. He (Dr Craven) would do that himself. He even went a bit further, because at the after-match function he made a sort of reserved, reluctant apology for his outburst at Newlands. Most of the British Press seemed unconvinced about the sincerity of the apology. That was followed by a statement which we understood had been written on behalf of Lochner absolving the Lions of sculduggery, saying that they played entirely within the spirit of Rugby Football, and what a charming bunch of fellows they all were! It was a complete contradiction, which left many people feeling rather confused.

It was because of these speeches that one or two members of the British Press wrote that the tour had turned sour, and made the accusation that the midweek South African sides were 'loaded' by adding top white players to the black and coloured teams simply in order to beat the Lions. However, in what was only an eighteen-match tour not all the provinces could play against the Lions. Some of the opposition had to be invitation sides, and had to include black and coloured players, so it was not always easy to be certain that the right men for the occasion were being chosen. If any criticism could be levelled at the team selection it was that too many players had three, four or five games against the Lions while others were not given any opportunity, although they may have been quite worthy of selection.

The South African Rugby Board could be criticized strongly for the way they were intending to select the South African Barbarians side for the match at Durban after the third Test. The Barbarians committee of three were going to have three Springbok selectors to join them, who were to have the casting vote. It meant that even the Barbarians were going to be chosen by the national selectors. That is of course completely contrary to the amateur spirit of Barbarians clubs in Britain, New Zealand, Australia, and also France, where Jean-Pierre Rives had started one. The whole concept is that they should be completely separate and autonomous, without any interference from an international body.

Fortunately Chick Henderson, who had managed the South African Barbarians in Britain, fought hard against the South African Board's idea, telling them in no uncertain terms what he thought about it. Dr Craven saw the red light, and decided that Henderson and his committee could choose the side.

16

The Second Test

For the Springboks the bitter memories of 1974 were fast
receding. Their 26–19 victory in the second Test at Bloemfontein
was even more convincing than the one at Newlands had been
a fortnight before. There were some remarkable similarities,
though. Six tries were scored – this time four by the Springboks
and two by the Lions. The first South African try, which again
came from a bad clearance, was scored by Rob Louw. At one
stage the Lions were 6–16 down; they improved that to 9–16
by half-time, and immediately afterwards kicked a penalty goal
to make it 12–16. All that was similar to the first Test.

There was also the customary injury which meant that the
Lions had to cope for the rest of the tour without their best
outside-half, Gareth Davies. Like his team-mate Terry Holmes,
he had torn knee ligaments. Both had also had dislocated
shoulders on the tour, and there was no guarantee that either
would be fit to play again by the following season.

So far as the result was concerned, the Lions could have no
complaints. They repeated their mistakes of the first Test; they
missed their tackles, they kicked badly, they were twice guilty
of crass stupidity which allowed an uncertain Naas Botha to
kick penalties. The game was only a few minutes old when
Andy Irvine kicked poorly out of defence, away from his
forwards and into the arms of Gerry Germishuys, the fastest
man on the field. From Germishuys the ball went to Morne du
Plessis and on to Louw. As he was tackled Louw passed to
Willie du Plessis, then got to his feet, took a return pass and
scored in the corner, too far out for Botha to convert.

The Lions' try not long afterwards was the result of a rare

Springbok error, Divan Serfontein fumbling a high kick by Colin Patterson, and John O'Driscoll, the best of the Lions forwards getting to the touchdown. Davies did what Botha had failed to do from the touchline, and the Lions were leading for the first and last time. The next twelve points all went to South Africa. Botha kicked a penalty goal after Graham Price climbed feet first into a ruck in full view of the referee. Then Theuns Stofberg scored a try, although we thought that in the build-up to it, Ray Mordt, beautifully tackled by Bruce Hay, had played the ball after it had touched the ground. Following that tackle there was some unbelievably poor tackling on Morne du Plessis and Stofberg who ran in behind the posts to give Botha an easy conversion. Botha also kicked a second penalty when Ray Gravell late-tackled David Smith. There was some excuse for Gravell. Earlier he had had a knock on the head and afterwards said that for most of the match he had been in 'Disneyland'. Perhaps he was happier there than his colleagues were on the field!

The forwards won a fair share of the ball but they lacked the control they had shown at Newlands. Two penalties on either side of half-time by the superbly cool Davies kept the Lions in the game, and when Irvine kicked a penalty goal from fifty-three metres there was only one point between the teams. At this point Davies had to go off and was replaced by Ollie Campbell, who was immediately given the opportunity to put the Lions ahead. Morne du Plessis, of all people, was the culprit. He had got off-side, and as he stood between the posts awaiting Campbell's kick he must have been thinking that if the ball went over the bar he would regret it to his dying day. He was spared that punishment. Campbell, kicking from an easy angle, hooked the ball past the post.

Perhaps it would have been better to have given the kick to Irvine, who at least was in tune with the match atmosphere. The truth was, though, that Irvine had been having a most unfortunate afternoon. Several times he was appallingly slack, and only once did he attempt to run at the opposition. The crowd, remembering him from six years ago, must have expected a much better performance. Still it was asking a lot of a man who was striving to get fully fit.

Hay twice saved tries, once with a tackle, and later intercepting in his own twenty-two and clearing to touch. Opposite him Mordt was giving a top-class performance and set up the try which turned the match. He ran down the right, and from the maul the ball went to Gysie Pienaar who was standing in the outside-half position. Pienaar, the outstanding player on the field, kicked for Germishuys on the left wing. The duel between the advancing Germishuys and the retreating John Carleton was won by Germishuys, amid tremendous Springbok rejoicing. A minute later Pienaar himself scored a try. The Lions passed the ball along their threequarter line, which for them was becoming quite a complicated manoeuvre, and Morne du Plessis was the first to the inevitable breakdown. He fly-kicked ahead and Pienaar won the chase. Botha converted this one from a wide angle, and the last-minute try to Gravell for the Lions certainly could not diminish the crowd's victory celebrations.

Jinx Strikes Again
by Carwyn James

The team who fail to profit from their mistakes hardly deserve to win. That the second Test was virtually a carbon copy of the first was a very poor reflection on the Lions. The Springboks had obviously decided that 'stop Patterson to stop Davies' was their best course of action, and so Patterson was put under such pressure that he made more mistakes than usual. While the Lions forwards held their own, they lacked the authority they had shown at Newlands, and the Springbok forwards had a little more of the aggressive animal instinct in the loose with Louw and Stofberg getting very quickly to the danger areas.

The first Springbok try was the result of the Lions' capacity for recurring instances of philanthropy, and the second the result of bad refereeing. I have no doubt that the ball touched the ground when Mordt was tackled, and that he was allowed to pass the ball off the ground. M. Palmade's error of judgement cost the Lions dearly. To give away one try and to be asked to concede another is not the way to win Tests.

Yet a side has to make its own luck, and somehow the Springboks managed to do that in both Tests. They showed a lively approach to the attacking and counter-attacking game, much of their thrust coming from their two strong-running wings and fullback. It was like watching Stanley Matthews and Stan Mortenson in the round ball game in the fifties. Attack hard on the wings, support, and then the openings are created in midfield. It is a refreshing style, and one which the Lions could not develop simply because they did not have the right players.

The Springbok selectors made their mistakes against the Jaguars. By the time they came to the Bloemfontein Test they had changed almost half the side. With a new fullback, a new centre and scrum-half, a new lock and a mobile front row, they looked a much better combination. What the Lions had failed to do was to force them into making selectorial errors. That was what the 1974 Lions had done. So, from then on, the 1980 Springbok selectors could sit back and even play their failures. I am certain that had they lost their first two Tests even Naas Botha, their 'golden boy' match-winner, would have been dropped.

In fact Botha was again disappointing in this match. The Lions' back row operated efficiently within the apron of the scrum but less so in the wider spaces. So Botha had plenty of freedom to move but he looked no more than a very ordinary club outside-half. On the Lions' side Davies was under much more pressure and showed himself to be in a much higher class. He can stretch for the ball and pass with his fingers in one stride, or, when he chooses, he can lean back and stroke the ball long distances. Davies is from the outside-half factory at Gwendraeth, where Barry John came from, and there is quite a lot of Barry John in Davies's play. His partnership with

Patterson could have developed into a great one like that of Kershaw and Davies, or Tanner and Davies. The Irish-Welsh alliance had all the ingredients of greatness. No touring team within my memory had been so struck by injuries, especially at half-back. They had been forced to play eight different half-back combinations in their first nine matches, so Davies's injury in this game was a very bitter blow. Later in the tour Patterson was injured too, so there was never a chance of realizing fully the potential of this talented pair.

Patterson, a solicitor, has an analytical mind which enables him to correct mistakes and improve his technique. In the first game of the tour he was too 'fussy', oscillating everywhere and nowhere, but against better opposition he had shown a very wide spectrum of ability. Jack McDowell, the former Irish international, had told Patterson 'Keep your arms close to your body and snap your wrists.' As a result he could move the ball without any perceptible back-swing. He always faces the opposition and so has a wide vision of the game, and is not so liable to be trampled on as many scrum-halves are. He is a stand-up player when he is passing, and so finds his partner much more easily. He is sure that the partners should be complementary, for each has an equal part to play. 'Gareth', he told me, 'is such a fine kicker that I think I always ought to give him a quick precise pass, but of course when I see there is pressure on him I know I must do something else.' He breaks very quickly in the set pieces, although early in his career he was inclined to do it too often; not so in his maturity.

The centres in this Test cancelled each other out. Woodward needed too much room to play in the centre at this level. Gravell had his impulsive moments, and tackled well if at times a little late, and the one 'ranji' he set up with Davies made the ideal platform from which the Lions should have scored. Repeated selfish attempts from three consecutive loose rucks by the back row and the scrum-half produced nothing. To hammer the opposition and to have no reward is psychologically damaging, and it was after this purple patch that the Lions conceded the second try. At 16–15 it was anyone's game, with the Lions looking more likely to win. Then the jinx struck again. Davies had to leave the field, and Campbell had the difficult task, with only thirteen minutes of play left, of being the general of the side. Worse still, coming in from the cold as it were, he was asked to make a crucial penalty shot which might well have clinched the game for his side. The ball veered away at the last moment and the game was lost. Pienaar was the man of the match, and it was he who delivered the coup de grace. He held the ball aloft in his moment of triumph, for the Springboks then could not lose the series.

The day before the match had been Friday the 13th, a dreadful day for the superstitious Rodney O'Donnell. By seven a.m. his team-mates were busy erecting ladders outside his bedroom door, putting down lines on the carpet, and pasting bits of paper bearing the number 13 on all the lift buttons. By that evening O'Donnell had lost his watch and his wallet. By the next evening the Lions had lost the crucial Test, and by the middle of the following week O'Donnell was lying in hospital with a dislocated neck. To some extent he had been lucky. The injury could have been very much worse. He was the eighth 'green bottle' to have fallen by the wayside accidentally since the tour had begun seven weeks before. It was incredible to realize that almost a third of the party had been wiped out by injury or illness. Their resilience was all the more remarkable.

17
Secret Training

On the Monday after the second Test defeat, the Lions, with their wounded, left for Johannesburg. It was a sad, sad day; not just because they had tasted failure again, but because they would have to say good-bye to four great players, Gareth Davies, David Richards, Terry Holmes, and Fran Cotton, who would depart for home. Their tour was over, and the Lions would feel their absence deeply as they soldiered on for seven more matches. On that Monday, too, Bill Beaumont could hardly make it to the bus. He had a bad knock on his knee, and it was full of fluid. There was another Lion with his hand bandaged. He had injured it in preventing a drunk from pestering Davies. So the injured pride limped on.

They were to play the Junior Springboks in Johannesburg, and they were astounded to find that their opponents had gone into hiding to conduct their preparation. What did they have to hide? Perhaps a new tactical plan to revolutionize the game; the unstoppable move. It seemed to this young Lions' party the height of absurdity, and certainly further evidence of an atmosphere that had no real part in the game of Rugby Football. Few of the Lions had been able to imagine beforehand how intense the approach to the game would be in South Africa.

Everyone knew, of course, that when the 1971 Lions returned from New Zealand they had been welcomed by a crowd of Beatle-like proportions. For the first time a series had been won, and the fame of Barry John, Gareth Edwards, Mervyn Davies and the rest spread throughout the world. Three years later the Lions' victory in South Africa confirmed the popularity of the game, and players realized that they stood in the world's gaze, and that they were under a pressure that had not existed previously. Most of the 1980 Lions had grown up in that sort of atmosphere, yet still they were amateurs, playing the game just because they loved it, and most of them had made sacrifices just to go on the tour. Still South Africa had surprised, perhaps even shocked some of them. Every day their activities on and off the field received equal treatment on the front pages of the newspapers with the most important matters of state. It hardly seemed proper, and when the Junior Springboks went into hiding, training in secret sessions, well, what could one do – laugh?

As a matter of fact the Junior Sprinkbok side looked quite good enough to win without going through all that secret palaver. The truth was that unless the Lions improved vastly on their midweek performances they would be in for a most unpleasant afternoon. Most of the opposition had played against them already. The captain, Wynand Claassen, was to make his third appearance against the Tourists. At tight-head was Hempies du Toit, who had given Fran Cotton so much trouble at Stellenbosch. The backs were certainly the most exciting the Lions had come up against. At scrum-half was Gawie Visagie, younger brother of the former Springbok outside-half, Piet. Gawie had been a very valuable member of the South African Barbarians in Britain, and his partner, Gavin Cowley, who had played in the Lions' first match, was most accomplished. In the centre were the young Western Province player Colin Beck, and Danie Gerber, a fine runner from Orange Free State. The wings were Derek Jeffrey, who had scored the best individual try of the tour against the Lions, and Darius Botha, the elder brother of the famous Naas. The fullback, Tim Cocks of Natal, was at the time reserve to the Springbok Gysie Pienaar. It was a very good side, certainly worthy of a Saturday game, and because of that the Lions had to strengthen their normal midweek XV. Three members of the Test pack were brought in, and a fourth was John O'Driscoll because Colm Tucker had sprained an ankle. Paul Dodge, who had joined the tour to replace Richards, was to make his first appearance. Elgan Rees was to play his first game for four weeks, and Andy Irvine was given the chance to find his feet after his unfortunate Test experience. He was to play on the right wing.

Two tries, one of them scored three minutes from full time and the other in the second minute of injury time, gave the Lions victory, but they could quite easily have lost. If the Junior Springboks' finishing had been anywhere near the standard of their approach work, then the Lions would have lost.

Again the Lions did not come through unscathed. Phil Orr left the field with a nasty gash in his left thigh, and Rodney O'Donnell left on a stretcher after a head-on tackle on Gerber. In deference to O'Donnell's superstitions, Gerber was wearing the number thirteen jersey. O'Donnell had dislocated his neck, which was bad enough, but it might have been worse. The habit of allowing ambulance men on to the field in South Africa and in New Zealand is of doubtful value. For minor injuries which just require the use of a sponge these worthy people perform a most useful function; for injuries of a more serious nature they are not equipped. By insisting that O'Donnell should move his neck they could easily have caused permanent damage. He could have been left paralysed. He was replaced by Clive Woodward, who was to play an important part in the result. He went to the left wing while Irvine moved to fullback.

Jim Renwick made it a bright opening by dropping a goal, but then the Lions lost so much pace that for a time they were close to complete disintegration. John Robbie and Tony Ward seemed unhappy in their partnership, and this was reflected in the rest of the backs. Du Toit did his best to collapse the scrums, and in fact if the Junior Springboks had not been so obsessed with trying to scrummage the Lions into the ground they might have done very much better. Visagie and Cowley formed the most lively half-back combination, and received excellent support from their back row, particularly from Geldenhuys, who had some measure of success in preventing the Lions from indulging in their favourite pastime of rolling the ball. It was Geldenhuys who scored the Springbok try, a try which Cowley converted, and at half-time they were well worth their three-point lead. It could have been more if they had kicked the three penalties awarded against the Lions.

With Irvine installed at fullback in the second half they looked more positive, because running from the deep was the Lions' most effective weapon. When Irvine crept up unnoticed on the blind side of the scrum he found to his great surprise an undefended route to the try-line. Ward, however, missed the simplest of conversions.

It was at this stage that the Junior Springboks demonstrated their inexperience, running well but passing badly. On one occasion Gerber dropped the ball inches from the Lions' line. A well-worked scissors between Renwick and Dodge enabled Rees to score a try. Woodward converted it and then combined beautifully with his Leicester clubmate Dodge, who scored the try which gave the Lions a margin of victory they had scarcely looked like achieving five minutes earlier.

For Dodge it was a successful Lions debut. He had stiffened the midfield and had played most sensibly. It was clear that the selectors would have to play him again on the following Saturday against Northern Transvaal.

On the way up to Pretoria for that match the rumour went round that Fergus Slattery had been asked to come to South Africa to replace O'Donnell. The unfortunate O'Donnell was in hospital undergoing an operation on his neck. It would be a long time before he played Rugby again. The management's decision to ask for a back row forward was understandable. The team's lack of pace in that area had proved to be a major problem both in attack and in defence, but the question in our minds was whether it was ethical to replace a fullback with a back row forward. It could be said that that was against the spirit of the tour agreement on replacements. It seemed that the management had abandoned the high principle they had maintained so far. The selection of the party as a whole had been well thought out. It was no coincidence that it had been one of the best behaved sides ever to have toured South Africa. That had been due to careful planning and to strong management; the players had responded well. However, asking for Slattery to replace O'Donnell seemed like lack of loyalty by the management to the players on the tour. In the event, things turned out for the best, because Slattery declined the invitation, and the Lions decided they were well enough served by the men they had. Some damage had been done, though. The South African Rugby Board had been generous and sympathetic on the question of replacements, and the Lions' management had shown that it was not only the Springboks who had an obsessive desire to win at all costs.

The Northern Transvaal match was the thirteenth of the tour. For weeks it had been referred to by the South Africans as the fifth Test. In truth for the Lions it was the thirteenth Test. Loftus Versfeld in Pretoria, where it was to be played, had been the scene of the Lions' greatest victory against the Springboks in 1974, but they had always found things much more difficult against the provincial side there. Only Andy Irvine had survived the passage of six years since the Lions' previous visit. In 1974 he had played on the wing; now he was at fullback with his countryman, Bruce Hay, on the wing. On the right wing was Clive Woodward, who developed into one of the most dashing runners in the side. Some people thought he ought to have been in the centre with his Leicester clubmate Paul Dodge. They had worked up a good understanding for their club and for England, and had shown that when they played against the Junior Springboks. Still the Lions' selectors persisted with Ray Gravell, who had been playing better in recent matches, although still prone to align badly in defence and to late-tackle, which was a liability. Gravell is a delightful man, and is constantly in need of reassurance about his game. When people told him that his best tackles were late ones, he always replied, 'I get there as quickly as I can.'

Derek Quinnell's absence from the side was significant. He had not been at all effective in the second Test, when his physical and mental hardness had not been sufficient to compensate for his lack of speed about the field. The back row was reorganized, with John O'Driscoll and Colm Tucker on the flanks and Jeff Squire at No. 8.

Four members of the Northern Transvaal pack had played for the Springboks in the second Test, and two others, Geldenhuys and the loose-head prop Jan Oberholtzer, had been in the Junior Springboks' pack. The team was captained by Naas Botha, playing in front of his own crowd and with his regular scrum-half, Tommy du Plessis. Here at last we expected to see the real Botha.

18
Pretorian Welcome

Pretoria gave the Lions the most enthusiastic welcome of the tour when they arrived there from Johannesburg two days before their match against Northern Transvaal – the 'Blue Bulls'. Pretoria is the seat of government for six months in the year, the other six months being spent in Cape Town. The good people of Pretoria marked the importance of their city, and the importance of the Lions' visit, by providing a cavalcade through the streets. The management and players were driven through the city in open vehicles accompanied by some lovely young ladies and cheered enthusiastically by thousands of onlookers.

Bill Beaumont shared a limousine with Naas Botha, the darling of South Africa, and the captain of the 'Blue Bulls'. Leading the parade was a white bull whose coat had been dyed blue especially for the occasion. He looked a little confused but behaved, well, and the whole turn-out was a great joy to the Lions. They loved it, as indeed they loved the whole of their stay in Pretoria.

The next day the Press were invited to lunch at the magnificent restaurant on the Loftus Versfeld ground where the match was to be played. The facilities at the ground were second to none that existed, and may only be surpassed by the new Ellis Park ground in Johannesburg when its reconstruction is complete. The pitch was in glorious condition, and in the dead-ball area a huge barbeton daisy, the emblem of Northern Transvaal, had been etched in yellow and red. The ground holds sixty-eight thousand, all seated, and for the match it was full, setting a world record for a provincial match. The Press, radio and television boxes are splendidly appointed, and altogether it is one of the finest grounds we have seen.

Maybe it was a coincidence that while the Four Home Unions were searching feverishly for a back row forward to help pull the Lions out of the mire, the back row who played at Loftus Versfeld put up the best show of the tour against the supposedly formidable 'Blue Bulls'. The Lions won this 'fifth Test' by 16–9, scoring all their points in the first half. Quite incredibly the penalty count against them in the second half was 10 to none, but just as incredibly the Lions did not allow the one-sided decisions given by the referee Freek Burger to upset them. Their first-half performance was certainly the best of the tour so far, particularly up front, where their power steadily wore down the much vaunted Northern Transvaal pack. The provincial front row spent most of the game in suspended animation, inelegantly perched on top of their opposite numbers.

Maurice Colclough and Bill Beaumont again lost the lineout battle by a considerable margin in the second half, but their work in the scrums and mauls had not been matched at any stage by South African forwards. The back row did most to set up victory. John O'Driscoll had not played better, and this time he received the support his hard toil deserved from Colm Tucker on the right flank and Jeff Squire at No. 8. Between them they put such pressure on the Northern Transvaal half-backs, Tommy du Plessis and Naas Botha, that the entire Northern Transvaal threequarter line was reduced to an incoherent rabble. They dropped passes, they collided with each other, and drew endless ribald remarks from their usually most devoted supporters.

The Lions had had a most debilitating effect on Botha. In the three matches he had played against them, this extraordinary goal-kicker had succeeded with only nine shots out of twenty-three. His handling and passing on the run were not in the same class as Gareth Davies's, and we thought that Botha did not yet possess the temperament for this class of football. Behind the driving force of Davies, John Robbie and Ollie Campbell were able to play with a composure that was denied to their counterparts. It was the tenth half-back partnership forced upon the Lions. In the absence of Colin Patterson, Robbie took the opportunity to close the gap on his rival in the contest for selection for the third Test. He had started a long way back, but by now there could be little in it. The speed and variety of Robbie's pass allowed Campbell enough room to run at the Northern Transvaal defence, and he played a most useful part in the Lions' second try, scored by Colclough after good build-up work by O'Driscoll and Tucker, and converted by Campbell. Still the Lions' threequarter line was not going as smoothly as it should at this stage of the tour, although Paul Dodge, with limited opportunities, played most sensibly. Clive Woodward on the wing had even fewer opportunities. He managed one or two twisting runs but confessed that his concentration lapsed during long spells of inactivity. Bruce Hay, on the other wing, with his basic training as a fullback, found more to occupy his time and did it to good effect. His running lacked the aesthetic quality of Woodward's, but was equally effective. One of his charges resulted in the scrum from which the Lions scored their first try, a pushover with Squire getting the credit for the touchdown. On either side of the Tourists' tries Andy Irvine kicked two monstrous penalty goals, the first after a lineout infringement from fifty-four metres, the second from sixty metres following a late tackle. As the referee only awarded penalties to the Lions inside their own half, it was as well for them that Irvine was present.

The crowd were urged repeatedly through the loudspeakers to shout their encouragement to their team, and there was an enthusiastic response from the flag-waving spectators, but their side never looked likely to get close enough to bother the Lions. They got nine points back in the second half with a dropped goal by Botha and a try by Tjokkie van der Merwe, which Botha converted, but that was all. As the game went on their forwards found it harder to get to the point of break-down, and this did nothing at all to promote the Test prospects of Thys Burger and Burger Geldenhuys. In fact neither was given a place in the Test side. The only change was at lock where Moaner van Heerden was brought back in place of Kevin de Klerk.

Forgotten Arts

by Carwyn James

The 'Blue Bulls' had been unbeaten in their last thirty-one matches, so they were attuned to the winning game, and I thought before the match that the Lions had only an outside chance of beating them. Attuned, well rehearsed, harmonizing beautifully, we were told, and well conducted by the young new maestro Botha; alas for the maestro and for his musical director, a most successful coach for many years, they misinterpreted their scripted score. They forgot the right tempo. Against other less endowed sides than the Lions they had no doubt set their own slow ponderous tempo. Their forwards looked just that – slow and ponderous – and when every now and again they were asked to raise a gallop, some of them got there and others did not. So, disunited they stood, and were led not as 'Bulls' but as stripling calves to the slaughter. I shall remember this game for the urgency, the drive and the will to win that the Lions showed in the first half. They were a motivated lot, determined to get on with the game, and whether they had the ability consciously to quicken the tempo or not, I do not know, but that is what they certainly did. It took the unthinking, unmusical Transvaalers from the North a long time to realize that they were not playing what they had practised, and these cheeky Lions tried things which lesser animals would not have dared at the home of the great Voertrekkers.

It leads me to write something about the forgotten arts of Rugby Football, and the overdone arts. Setting the tempo of the game is not so much a forgotten art as one never really appreciated by many. When the Lions, midway through the first half on the hard-baked ground of the High Veldt, kept the ball at their feet, I imagined we were back at Murrayfield in the mid-thirties with the cries of 'Feet, feet!' echoing through the stadium. It was all imagination, because by this time the sixty-eight thousand people at Loftus Versfeld were reduced to silence, and some perhaps even to tears. The Lions, however, perhaps more by accident than by design, had dribbled the ball a full thirty metres right into the 'Blue Bulls' twenty-two, and there were the 'Bulls' at sixes and sevens desperately trying to find a counter to an art form which they may never have seen. So foreign is this forgotten art of dribbling to South African Rugby that I did not see a single reference to it in the scores of articles written about the game.

Another is the cross-kick. With wings such as Hay lacking in pace, the obvious substitute for running is the cross-kick. Properly executed it can be a lethal weapon, and the Lions used it expertly. With the ball ascending to dizzy heights they could take advantage of the keen atmosphere and the glare of the sun in a sky as blue as the Mediterranean in midsummer.

Another forgotten art was in evidence throughout the match – Botha's inability and that of his threequarters to pass the ball at speed. Theirs were pathetic attempts at an art which is absolutely basic to the game of Rugby Football. For that reason alone I was delighted to see the Lions giving a cocky winning team the lesson of their lives. Rugby is not about a big dominating pack winning possession at will and plying their halves with kickable ball. Week after week we had heard of the victories gained by Northern Transvaal, with perhaps a try or maybe two, but mainly through the boot of Botha, who usually manages a hat-trick of dropped goals.

This leads me to the overdone arts. In this game, and indeed in too many of the games I had seen in South Africa, far too many attempts had been made to drop goals. It is of course the easiest way of scoring points and winning matches. In 1948 the value of the dropped goal was reduced from four points to three, and I sincerely hope that soon the International Board will reduce this prostituted art to two points. This is more relevant in South Africa than elsewhere, but it applies wherever the game is played.

The men of the match for me were the two No. 8s, Squire and Johann Marais. Marais figures in my second plea to the International Board concerning the value of the penalty kick. Lying off a maul, Marais was quick to reach Campbell in a defensive position well within his twenty-two, gathering a typically accurate pass from Robbie. Campbell, as usual, cradled the ball with care and kicked it well down the field without finding touch. Marais arrived as soon as he could, but, justly as the referee thought, marginally too late. The penalty was awarded to the Lions where the ball landed, and in any case fifteen metres in from touch as the law demands. Irvine with a prodigious kick of sixty-five metres put the ball between the posts. So from a difficult defensive position for the Lions one marginally late tackle gave them three points. What kind of ball game were we playing? Compare those three lucky points with the four which a team wins when the ball has passed maybe through thirty pairs of hands. Rugby Football, after all, is a handling running game, yet games are still being won by great kickers.

In South Africa Botha is the new golden boy. By world standards he is a very ordinary outside-half. He certainly was never from the mould of Barry John – who incidentally had arrived in time to see this game. He too was singularly unimpressed by Botha's general play, and even by his kicking. Botha may yet develop into a reasonable club outside-half, but youngsters can only emulate him for his magnificent kicking. If South Africa are to turn out a conveyor-belt series of kicking outside-halves then I can only weep for them. In this game there was too much pressure on Botha. He was only twenty-two, and recently he had been made captain of his province. Great pressure was on him to win the match. He failed with his first kick, and then with his second, and in the whole game he could manage only an easy conversion and a dropped goal from a free kick. The new-look Lions' back row put pressure on him, and it was the first time on the tour that I had seen him collared and scragged and looking much the worse for wear. His displays so far against the Lions having been sub-standard, I was prompted to say over the air that he had not got the big-match temperament.

Colclough gave another stunning performance for the Lions, and his try, a stirring run from the twenty-two metre line, was the result of imaginative play by the Irish trio, O'Driscoll, Tucker and Campbell. A good week for the lads! These were two important victories.

Ollie the Fisherman

Everyone was glad to have the three days' holiday in Durban before the third Test. None more so than Ollie Campbell, who with Alan Tomes got up at six o'clock to go on a fishing trip. Tomes was a most enthusiastic fisherman; not so most of the others who went on this particular trip. The water was rather choppy and they were violently sick. While Campbell was hanging over the side of the boat feeling like death warmed-up he felt a tug on his rod. In spite of all his troubles he hauled in his line and what should be on the end of it but a twenty-six-pound barracuda! No one was more surprised than Ollie – except possibly the barracuda.

Apart from the break in training, for which was substituted golf, tennis, swimming and just lying on the beach, the players got away from the Press. This was a welcome relief because they had not been out of the public gaze for seven weeks. But while the rest of the Lions were enjoying themselves in Durban, Rodney O'Donnell was recovering from an operation in the Rand Clinic in Johannesburg. 'I am lucky to be alive,' he told his visitors. 'Thank God John O'Driscoll was playing. He stopped the first aid men from straightening my neck.'

O'Donnell had a bone grafted from his hip to repair the damaged fifth vertebra. On the Tuesday of that week he was a little sad because the specialist had just told him he was not fit enough to travel to Port Elizabeth for the third Test. He wanted to rejoin the Lions, but he would not be fit to travel for some time. The sad youngster from Dublin with the soft voice knew another door in his life had been closed. 'I shall never play again,' he said. That night Dr Jack Matthews spent a couple of hours persuading him that he could not possibly rejoin the tour.

When the party came to leave Durban they were held up for two hours at the airport because the plane to take them to Port Elizabeth had been held up by foul weather in the Cape. This weather was making its way to port Elizabeth in time for the Test.

19
The Third
Test

On the morning of the third Test Bill Beaumont looked out of his bedroom window in Port Elizabeth, and must have thought it was going to be the Lions' day. The rain poured down, and it made him very happy. Noel Murphy was happy too, but he prayed that there would be no wind. He knew the Lions had to apply a continuous pressure on the Springboks and that would be very difficult in a raging wind favouring one side continuously for forty minutes. In the event there was quite a lot of wind.

The Lions had picked the side originally chosen for the Northern Transvaal match at Pretoria, which meant that Colin Patterson was back at scrum-half. John Robbie had been brought in at Pretoria because Patterson was then unfit. Robbie had played well in that match, but Patterson had played well in his matches too, except in the second Test when he took one or two wrong options, and it would have been unkind to have dropped him. Overall the side showed five changes from the second Test, two of them positional. The three newcomers were Paul Dodge, in the centre in place of his Leicester clubmate, Clive Woodward, who moved to the right wing displacing John Carleton; Ollie Campbell, at outside-half in place of Gareth Davies, by then back in Wales; and Colm Tucker on the flank, with Jeff Squire moving to No. 8 in place of Derek Quinnell. So Quinnell's previous unfitness had allowed the current back row to establish their claim successfully. Quinnell and Carleton were the two to be dropped, and both were naturally disappointed, but Carleton was also upset because no one had told him why he had been dropped. He had played very bravely in the second Test, having had a sprung rib cartilage only ten days previously. He did nothing particularly wrong in that game and had been a most loyal member of the party. As it turned out the absence of an experienced wing was to cost the Lions dear.

Morne du Plessis won the toss and chose rather strangely to play into the wind and the rain. After a minute that did not seem a very good idea because Ollie Campbell, who had been injured in a late tackle, kicked a penalty goal for the Lions. It was the first time they had scored first in a Test. However, it soon became obvious that little had changed since the day when the Lions had returned from their unsuccessful venture to New Zealand in 1977. For fourteen weeks on that tour they had subjected their opponents to every possible indignity. In the final Test at Eden Park there had been times when the All Blacks went into the scrums with only three forwards in order to avoid protracted physical confrontation.

The All Blacks had won the match, though, and with it the series, because of the failure of the Lions' backs. It had been an unreal experience for those who had for so many years witnessed the domination of the All Blacks' forwards, but had been thrilled by the genius of the Lions' backs. Three years on, it was the same story in South Africa. Perhaps we had become so obsessed with the importance of forward play in Britain that we had completely overlooked the importance of the backs. Perhaps the golden rule of coaching, 'Win the forward battle and win the match', had persisted long enough, for on the evidence of what had happened in New Zealand and in South Africa it was patently not true.

The Lions in this third Test won at a conservative estimate sixty-five per cent of possession from lineouts, rucks and mauls. It was only in the scrum that the Springboks could break even. Again the Lions defeat by 12–10 was due to the total inability of the backs to take the chances that were so frequently presented. Even allowing for the wet and windy conditions, some of the handling was sub-standard. With the line open ahead of them, both Dodge and Andy Irvine spilled passes; neither was easy, but at this level the half-chance is very often the only one. The best opportunity fell to Patterson, who spent much of his time, as he had done at Bloemfontein two weeks earlier, making the wrong decisions. With the Lions leading 10–6 and the game in the final quarter, another ruck was won by the Lions inside the Springboks' twenty-two. Patterson swung right down the narrow side, and with Ray Gravell, who had managed to work up a full head of steam, and Woodward outside him, Patterson chose to take on the two defenders himself. One into two just did not go.

Even at that stage the Lions had such a tight grip on things that if the Springboks were to score a try it would have to come from a mistake by the Lions. So it did. The Lions were obliging to the end. Naas Botha, who had played well under far greater pressure than he had experienced in the first two Tests, kicked low diagonally over Woodward's head. The ball skidded off the slippery surface and rolled so close to touch that Woodward, with Gerry Germishuys immediately behind him, could only put it into touch. An experienced wing would have booted the ball into the back row of the stand, but Woodward allowed Germishuys to grab the ball and throw it in quickly to the waiting Theuns Stofberg, whose legs on this occasion had worked every bit as fast as his brain. With no one to challenge him, Germishuys took the return pass from Stofberg and scored his third successive Test try.

Next to Gysie Pienaar, Germishuys had been the most influential Springbok of the series. The kick from the touchline may have been an important one as far as the winning of the match was concerned, but a draw would be enough to make the series safe for the Springboks. Botha's kick, with a saturated ball, was a beauty.

The Lions had one more chance – a penalty awarded near the touchline on the Springboks' twenty-two. Campbell, who had missed an equally crucial kick in the second Test from about the same position on the left hand side of the field, was called up. He had hooked the kick at Bloemfontein; this time there was no curl on the flight of the ball and it sailed past the post on the far side. With two minutes left even the forwards were resigned to the fact that the Lions were destined to lose, although everything had been in their favour.

Apart from Campbell's penalty kick in the first half Bruce Hay scored a try, picking up a loose clearance by Divan Serfontein, and going over in much the same place as Germishuys was to score later in the game. Naas Botha scored a penalty goal in the first half, and even when he brought the Springboks within a point of the Lions immediately after half-time with a dropped goal, there was no cause for alarm from the Lions' point of view. Campbell kicked another penalty goal and the Lions pressed for a decisive score. The opportunities came, slipped by, and the score, when it arrived, was at the other end.

So South Africa had for the first time won the first three Tests against the Lions, and were looking forward to Pretoria for the grand slam. The only incentive left to the Lions was to avoid a whitewash.

So Unlike Pontypool Rugby

by Carwyn James

The sheets of cold rain that fell on the Boet Prasmus Stadium made it look like Pontypool Park, only the Lions dillied and dallied for the first quarter playing anything but Pontypool Rugby. When they settled down to play a tighter game they forced Serfontein into error which brought a gift try for Hay. The second half was reminiscent of the first Test with the Lions' forwards firmly in control. Colclough dominated the lineout, upsetting the two-handed catching of Louis Moolman, and playing well in harmony with Beaumont – Colclough deflecting and Beaumont clearing up. Sometimes the technique was reminiscent of the double banking lineout system of the early sixties. Squire was prominent at the tail, setting up the powerful peels.

The rolling maul was not as effective as usual because the roll did not carry far enough, and because of the slowness of delivery, and however well it was controlled, Louw and Stofberg were able to lie up as stoppers to prevent movements at source. The roll was much more productive when Squire or Beaumont took the ball on the charge. Again chances were lost and one given.

When the ball went out of play I felt uneasy, because the ball boys always had another ball ready. The law states that a quick throw must be taken with the same ball, but I remember a provincial side in New Zealand scoring a try from a quick throw using another ball. The Lions may not have been conversant with the law on this point, for Woodward, a centre playing on the wing, gently shepherded a well-placed diagonal kick from Botha into touch, and from it South Africa got a soft try.

On this unreal tour it was inevitable that the Lions should give away one try, just as Botha would emerge as the match-winner. Ten points apiece, and as if defying the law of gravity, and the gravity of the situation, the heavy slippery ball cleared the cross-bar. The Lions could offer no excuses. They had to realize and accept the fact that back play in Britain had deteriorated beyond belief during the last decade. They hardly ran on to the ball, a fault apparent in the half-back play, and since the opposition did not pay too much attention to the hindmost foot law at the scrums, rucks and mauls – they were allowed to lie up in off-side positions – the threequarters found it difficult to make any progress. Irvine was hardly used as an attacker, and the lack of pace or guile on the wings meant that the Lions had to play a limited game. They preferred to play the ball back to their strength, which was obviously the forwards.

From the Springboks' point of view it is only fair to say they made their mistakes before the Lions arrived. They made mistakes in selection of the team to play in the first Test and even in the second against the Jaguars. Once they had seen their deficiencies they were quick to find another fullback, another centre and another scrum-half. They changed the composition of the front row and went for mobility, because it was generally accepted in New Zealand circles that the presence of people like

Johann Strauss, although he was retained as a replacement for some of the Test matches against the Lions, did not give the pack a great deal of mobility. So changes were made. A new hooker was found in Kahts, and a new tight-head prop, and Stofberg was given his opportunity to play on the flank.

In Pienaar they had found a winner. After three Tests he showed that he was as good as anyone in the world. His predecessor Edwards, whom we had seen playing for Northern Transvaal, was nowhere near his class. It was fascinating to know that at the end of the previous season in South Africa the Rugby journalists, when asked to give their votes for the best fullback, had voted by about ten to one for Edwards. So Pienaar burst on to the scene, showed that he was an attacking fullback, ever ready to run the ball, and made life very difficult for the Lions who tried to kick into the blank spaces. Pienaar usually managed to collect the ball, and although many people criticized him at the beginning and said that he was the type of fullback who made mistakes, that certainly was not the case. I would have said after three Test matches that he could have been awarded the man of the match prize for each of the games. For me, certainly, he was the man of the series. When you realize that the Lions were struggling in the fullback position at the beginning of the tour, it was a fine bonus point for the Springboks to have discovered, perhaps by chance, a fullback with the talents that Pienaar obviously had.

They were also well equipped on the wings to play the game the Lions could not possibly play. They had speed and strength – Mordt was a very strong runner. When they set up attacks on the periphery, with Louw, Morne du Plessis and Stofberg in support, they could set up loose rucks and whip the ball out to the other wing. We did not see a great deal of that type of game in the third Test, it is true, but it was always there for the Springboks to utilize. What in fact happened was that they held on like grim death. Morne du Plessis, a good leader, knew that he was playing in a beaten pack, but he kept them going really well. When Germishuys scored his try it was obvious they would fight to the death.

Still it was a lucky victory for the Springboks. I had no doubt about that. Neither had Morne du Plessis. But the fact is that the Lions did not score tries when they had the opportunities, and at this level the side winning good possession should be able to score points.

20
Hugo
Porta

Hugo Porta, the Barry John of the present era, returned to King's Park Durban on the first Wednesday in July to bring a new concept to the Rugby we had been watching in South Africa. He had played there a couple of months before for South America against the Springboks. Then he was not himself, not the amazing maestro who had led Argentina in Britain, for he was still suffering from an injury. The South African Barbarian selectors knew this, and they knew what joy to lovers of the game a fit Porta could bring. So they enticed him back for their match against the Lions. What a brilliant thought it was! Although the Lions won 25–14 the greatest enjoyment of the afternoon was the sight of this magnificent artist from Argentina prompting those around him to accomplish deeds of which they could scarcely have imagined themselves capable. There was limited possession on which he could work, yet he was always making something out of nothing, finding gaps that did not exist, bringing out undiscovered talents – those of the coloured Errol Tobias, for example, who played behind him in the centre – or prompting the others with a chip or grubber through the defence.

He shone as a diamond in the colourful setting of this intimate stadium, the crowd were thrilled by his skill, and no one enjoyed it more than Barry John himself.

For the Lions' XV that day it was a privilege to play against him. Afterwards Ollie Campbell and Gareth Williams, the open-side wing forward, were fulsome in their praise for the man they had been trying to stop during that humid afternoon. Porta's performance in fact served to highlight the lack of skill outside the scrum in the Lions' play throughout the tour, and indeed in that of the Springboks in the Tests. Had Porta been on either side in the Test series, his performance would undoubtedly have been decisive.

His skill lay first of all in his positioning. When scrums were formed either tight or loose he varied the distance, and in fact the angle at which he stood in relation to his partner Ian Buchanan. Sometimes he was so close that Mark Loane, the Australian playing at No. 8, could support him, or he could run in an arc and straighten up to set his threequarters going with a fall-away pass. His changes of pace were a constant puzzle to the Lions' back row. Sometimes he would make a swift break with his startling acceleration, and then Tobias would have his chance to give the Lions an object lesson in straight running.

Unlike many outside-halves throughout the ages Porta is an uncompromising tackler. He stopped Andy Irvine from scoring a certain try. Inevitably though for his position the judgement of his class depends almost entirely on how he attacks, and Porta's attack was as varied as the colours in a rainbow. He appeared everywhere, inside the wing, or supporting the outside centre, and then, just like John Dawes, he had the uncanny knack of finding the right man for the pass. Nearly all his passes provided great opportunities for the recipients. From a set piece he could motivate his threequarter line at such speed that his opponents looked slow and cumbersome.

Porta considers kicking a minor art. He likes the running game, and here, in the ideal conditions at Durban, he ran and handled with skill and enjoyment. Yet his kicking could hardly be faulted. Using his right foot most of the time, he never wasted a yard when kicking down the line. Once he put an up-and-under in motion with perfect judgement, and his chips to the corridor between the threequarters and fullback gave every chance to his centres. Like all great ball players he was unhurried. Watching him was like watching the graceful stroke-play of a master batsman. Porta, above all others, restored our faith in the aesthetic and artistic possibilities of backplay, which the Lions were ignoring so disappointingly.

The game was hectic but always entertaining, for indeed Porta seemed to bring the best out of the Lions too. John Robbie was dominant at scrum-half for the Lions, always probing, feeding and looking as complete a footballer as Porta himself. John Carleton, played on the left wing instead of the right, where Elgan Rees could not quite make as much of his chances as Carleton did. Jim Renwick still lacked confidence but had some bright moments, while Irvine ran superbly yet tackled badly. He got up with Carleton on one occasion and outran the defence to score a try.

However, even the dazzling Porta could not dim the brilliance of Tony Ward's performance. Ward, who had been rescued when in difficulties in the Indian Ocean the day before, was outstanding in the Lions' side. He scored seventeen points with a try, two conversions and three penalty goals. Maybe there were times when he hung on to the ball too long, but he and Robbie made sure for once that the splendid work of the Lions' forwards was not completely wasted, as it so often had been.

Still the criticism could be made that they ought to have scored more tries than they did, had this been a day for criticism. But it was not, for everyone at King's Park that day must have been more than satisfied with what they saw. By half-time the Lions had scored nineteen points to six. Ward had kicked his three penalty goals and converted the try when Alan Tomes, who had his best game of the tour, barged over the line, and Irvine had scored his try. Tobias, revelling in Porta's promptings, paved the way for a try by Frankie Davids which Porta converted.

Solomon Mhlaba, the Barbarians' black fullback, tore his knee ligaments and had to be replaced by Gawie Visagie, which did no harm to the Barbarians' game. Loane, who was leading the Barbarians, scored the best try of the match after a magnificent solo run. He had been in splendid form throughout. Then Ward scored his try for the Lions, following a hefty scrummage shove. Finally the Lions won a scrum on their own line, and Buchanan nipped in ahead of Robbie to touch down at John Beattie's feet. It was the only time Robbie had failed. No one could grumble. Six tries had been scored, and the game had provided the best entertainment of the tour, all in the finest traditions of Barbarian Rugby.

By then the Lions' thoughts were turning towards home. There were ten days to go, but their momentum had to be maintained. They may have lost the Test series, but they could still win the last one, and they must strive to keep their provincial record intact. With these thoughts they travelled to Cape Town again.

After the Barbarians game the Lions had had to say 'Farewell' to the unfortunate Rodney O'Donnell. His neck was in a brace following the dislocation he had suffered a fortnight before. Before he left for Johannesburg to catch the plane home he noted that his neck harness had thirteen holes punched in it. The superstitious O'Donnell was always discovering some new terror. While he was flying home, the Lions were in their plane to Cape Town and were given a rare treat. The pilot said he had made up some time and in honour of the Lions he would make a detour round Table Mountain. As they looked down on the magnificent scenery many of his passengers agreed that Cape Town was indeed the most beautiful city in the world.

At the foot of the Mountain is Newlands, where the Lions had lost the first Test. It is overlooked by Devils Peak, and if the Lions on their first visit had thought that name ominous, this new and unusual view from the air must have inspired them, for two days later against Western Province on that same Newlands ground they achieved their biggest victory of the tour.

The selectors decided to leave Clive Woodward out for this game. His inexperience on the wing had led to the winning Springboks try in the second Test, yet he had proved to be the most talented runner in the party except for Andy Irvine, and at that time he was top points scorer. John Carleton was retained on the wing, a strong pointer to the choice for the last Test in Pretoria. Irvine was again included; it would be his sixth consecutive game, but in fact Irvine was injured towards the end of the match and Woodward went on as his replacement. Apart from Woodward, and with John Robbie at scrum-half instead of Colin Patterson, it was the side who had lost the third Test, and presumably, barring accidents, it would be the side for the fourth Test. Whether Robbie could have saved the third Test is a matter for argument which can never be settled, but he would probably have let the ball go much more than Patterson. Robbie had brought more out of his partners than Patterson had done, and the speed with which he could get the ball away was a vital factor when the forwards did not seem to be releasing it until the last possible moment. His pass was certainly the fastest of any of the scrum-halves who had played.

For a change the Lions' opponents had injury problems. Their captain, Morne du Plessis, had very bad toothache and his face was so swollen that he had to withdraw from the match. He had been suffering with it since the day before the third Test. In addition the Province's international outside-half Robbie Blair could not play, so the Springboks' scrum-half Divan Serfontein had another partner. It meant the reorganization of their back division. They were joint holders of the Currie Cup and were the last major provincial side to challenge the Lions' unbeaten record outside the Tests.

21
Campbell's Twenty-Two Points

The dentist who had performed the operation on Morne du Plessis's wisdom tooth reckoned he had done the Lions a great favour. We met this dentist on the flight from Cape Town to Kimberley after the Western Province match. He said that it was because of his work inside the mouth of du Plessis that the Western Province captain was unable to lead his side and the Lions had had their biggest victory of the tour. We may not have succeeded in disillusioning the good dentist, but the fact was that it was du Plessis to whom he had done the favour. It was a good match for him to miss. His side were so completely outplayed that it is doubtful whether even he could have reduced the margin of their defeat.

It hardly needs saying that the Lions' forwards were in complete command. They scarcely did anything wrong. Remarkably, this technically unblemished performance was given against the five front forwards who had played in the ugly match at Stellenbosch five weeks earlier. Derek Quinnell, the captain on that day, had said afterwards that the Lions would look forward to meeting them again, and that was an ominous statement. There were certainly one or two petty squabbles during the match between the front rows, but the Lions' play so overwhelmed the Province pack that they could ride these little upsets without any distraction at all.

The only disappointing feature so far as the Lions were concerned was that with almost unlimited possession – the lineout was their weakest point – they could score only three tries, two of those coming from their opponents' mistakes. Even at the time of their greatest success the story of their play was on the same theme all through; the backs just were not fully complementary to the forwards. In fact the score of 37–6 by which they won was more a reflection of Ollie Campbell's accurate kicking than anything else. He scored a total of twenty-two points with four penalty goals, two dropped goals and two conversions. This took him above Woodward as the Lions' top scorer, and they finished in that order at the end of the tour. Woodward, in fact, did get a few points from the match, because in the last quarter he had to go on to replace Andy Irvine, who had pulled a leg muscle. Woodward, running in splendid style, scored the last try.

Irvine had played well, giving great attacking support to Bruce Hay on the left wing. Irvine scored a try on the right, though, when he was able to finish off a move started by John Carleton after the Province passing broke down. This usually happened on the few occasions when the Province were in possession. Carleton put in an excellent run before handing on to the swerving Irvine.

In the first half Irvine had scored a dropped goal. Campbell had already kicked two dropped goals and then a penalty goal, so the Lions led by 12–3 at half-time, Colin Beck, the outside-half substitute for Blair, having kicked a penalty goal for the Province. Campbell, with another penalty goal, and Hay, with a try, sealed the Province's fate. Hay's try was again the result of a Western Province mistake. Their fullback Frik Naude gave a badly timed pass which Hay anticipated and intercepted perfectly, before running fifty metres to score. Campbell converted that, kicked two more penalties, and converted Irvine's try before Divan Serfontein kicked a penalty goal for the Province. Woodward's try came after three well-won rucks, and certainly was the best of the day.

In spite of the paucity of tries the Lions' performance was most heartening, this being the probable side for the last Test. The back row, John O'Driscoll, Colm Tucker and Jeff Squire, had actually played better than in their fine performance in the third Test. Squire had a wonderful time in the lineout. Gelden-huys, who was deputizing for Morne du Plessis, stood at the back and the Province constantly threw the ball to him, but he was no match for Squire. The Province's biggest man, Hennie Bekker, stood at No.2, and they hardly ever threw for him. The two front rows finished their extended duel with honours about even.

Robbie had certainly played himself into the last Test, and that was a good sign for Campbell, who was beginning to prosper at the end of Robbie's swift pass. Campbell showed in this game why the Irish selectors preferred him to Ward. He has rather more all-round skill, and he reads a game better than Ward, even if Ward is often a match-winner. The impression one gets when watching Ward play is that he is a Soccer man first and a Rugby man second. After this game the selectors confirmed their intention to play Robbie at scrum-half in the final Test, by naming Colin Patterson for the position in the next game against Griqualand West at Kimberley.

While the team went to Kimberley, Irvine went on to Johannesburg to receive treatment for his various leg injuries. In addition to an achilles tendon strain he had aggravated his hamstring injury. The management seemed confident that he would be fit for the fourth Test, but in fact he had not been one hundred per cent fit since he arrived in South Africa.

The Last Replacement

Kimberley, the diamond town, flourished at the very beginning of South African Rugby history. It was a Mr Percy Ross Frames of Kimberley who took the first action towards forming the South African Rugby Football Board. Kimberley had sent a team in 1888 to tour Western Province, and there had been arguments because of different interpretations of the laws. In Cape Town Mr Frames found a Mr W. M. Bisset to support him in his idea of forming an overall ruling body. When some of the men who had most to do with the game talked about it, they agreed informally that the first president should be nominated by the centre where the next tournament was to take place, and that was Kimberley. So Mr Frames became the first President of the Board, which was established in 1889.

Two years later the first British touring side, W. E. Maclagan's team, included Kimberley in their itinerary, and in fact played what would now be called a Test match there. They also played against Griqualand West 'on a ground absolutely destitute of grass, hard, and covered with reddish dust'. Paul Clauss, a Scottish international who was one of the backs on that tour, wrote: 'Frequently one lost sight of the ball in the pillars of dust that rose up in the wake of the players as they ran. Under the circumstances the play was chiefly confined to the forwards, especially so in the game against Griqualand West.'

Before the team left England Sir Donald Currie (then Mr Currie), the founder and chairman of the Castle Shipping Line, gave Maclagan a gold cup to be presented to the team who put up the best game against them. That proved to be Griqualand West, who were beaten by only a converted try to nil. A try in those days counted one point, and a converted try three points. So at the end of their tour, in which they played nineteen matches and won them all, Maclagan's team had a farewell lunch on board the Garth Castle in Cape Town, and Maclagan presented the cup to the Griqualand West officials. At once they offered it to the South African Rugby Board as a challenge cup to be competed for every year by the provinces in South Africa. They still compete for the Currie Cup.

In those early days Griqualand West had supplied the majority of players to what came to be recognized as the national side, and although the province has had its ups and downs it has continued to produce players of international class. In recent years we remember Mannetjies Roux, that volatile centre, and Piet Visagie, a member of Dawie de Villiers's side who toured Britain in 1969. Piet's young brother, Gawie, was in the team against the Lions, in fact making his third appearance against them. He played for the Junior Springboks at scrum-half and then for the South African Barbarians at Durban, when he went on at fullback for the injured Mhlaba. The previous season, Griqualand West had run Western Province very close in the Currie Cup, but in 1980 they were apparently not so good, and lost to Boland. As Gareth Williams, who had been suffering from a stomach ailment, was by now able to train without discomfort, he was included against Griqualand to give Colm Tucker a rest. For those who turned out it was their last game of the tour and naturally they were keen to preserve the provincial record.

In the event is was a game to be missed. The play was untidy, the sides were not very good-tempered, and Colin Patterson was carried off in the first half with torn knee ligaments.

This was extremely serious because it meant that there was no cover at scrum-half for the Test. It had already been decided to play John Robbie, but if he were injured there was no specialist to replace him. So the call went out for yet another replacement. He would have to sit on the bench for the final Test and might not get a game, but the management felt that the risk of being without cover could not be taken. So Steve Smith, the England scrum-half from Sale, flew out, and sat on the bench for the whole of the Test. 'I suppose I shall just be a trick question in future sports quizzes', he said.

The Lions just managed to win by 23–19 against Griqualand West. No one could be happy about the game. The Lions allowed themselves to be chased around for a long time. Fist fights broke out at fairly frequent intervals, and van Tonder, the Griquas' lock forward, seemed fortunate to escape being sent off for putting the boot in. The refereeing was of such poor quality that the game threatened to run out of control.

For once the Lions' forwards were not in command. They were lethargic and showed no real enthusiasm for the job, but John Beattie got an early try. Bruce Hay cut through the defence after a scissors with Tony Ward, and Ian Stephens, taking the ball on, fed Beattie at just the right moment.

Possibly the best feature of the game was the play of the Griquas' scrum-half, Gawie Visagie. He had a splendid game.

He worked out a try for his side soon after Beattie's try, Oosthuizen, the No. 8, being the scorer, and Visagie converted it. Then he and Ward swapped penalty goals. Derek Quinnell, the Lions' captain for the day, spent half-time trying to straighten things out with the referee, and it seemed he had done some good, because the second half was much better. Visagie put his side furthur ahead with another penalty goal, but after that the Lions' pack showed more control. Tries came from John Robbie, who had come on for the injured Patterson, and from Peter Morgan, and both of them also dropped goals. Clive Woodward opened the way for Morgan's try, which Ward converted. Woodward still looked worth a place in the Test side, but where could they play him? The Lions looked to be safe by this time and they relaxed, and were punished for it. Visagie kicked another penalty goal, and in injury time Koch, a flank forward, scored a try for Griqualand West. The only satisfactory feature from the Lions' viewpoint was that they maintained their provincial unbeaten record and they were only the second British Isles team to achieve that in this century.

We had hoped that for the last Test the Lions' selectors would have taken a calculated risk and filled their back division with the best runners they had, to run hard at the South African defence, which had never been fully tested. The selection of John Robbie was a good start for that policy, but they would also have to have Woodward. Robbie's selection was inevitable because Colin Patterson was in hospital, having his severed knee ligaments sewn up and wondering whether he would be able to play again. Even if Patterson had been fit, though, Robbie would surely have been given the place. However, they left out Woodward, so it seemed that the Lions would persist to the last with the crash-ball charging in the middle, and the occasional thrust on the wing by Irvine. If those tactics failed – and they usually did – they would just have to hope that one of the backs would kick accurately at every opportunity.

This was a policy that had transformed Gerry Germishuys from an uncoordinated sprinter into a national hero, Gysie Pienaar from a good provincial fullback into possibly the best fullback in the world, and Naas Botha from a mediocre outside-half into a survivor of the Tests. Bill Beaumont agreed that the South African backs left a lot to be desired, yet they had scored ten tries in three matches, even while their forwards had been completely outplayed. The series had defied all the preconceived principles of international Rugby.

The Springboks had to keep Ewoud Malan as their hooker because Willie Kahts was not fit. Malan, who was Kahts's deputy in the Northern Transvaal side, had been capped as a replacement when Kahts was injured in the third Test. Morne du Plessis, the captain of South Africa, was fit again to lead his side after his wisdom tooth trouble.

So the Lions began the last stage of their seven thousand mile journey through South Africa, flying from Kimberley to Johannesburg in about fifty-five minutes. Eighty-nine years before, Maclagan's team had done this stage in reverse, travelling part of the way in coaches, each drawn by ten ponies, and the remainder by train. They reached their destination at eleven o'clock in the evening of the third day of travelling, thoroughly exhausted, and played a match the next day! After an hour's bus ride from Johannesburg, the Lions were in Pretoria with ample time to prepare for their last match three days later.

Press conference: Syd Millar talks to some of the largest Press party ever to follow a Lions tour, while the players train at Newlands for the First Test. Chris Rea, in the front of the picture on the left has his hand to his mouth, and Carwyn James stands on the extreme right. BELOW Graham Price, spearhead of the wedge, is driven on by Jeff Squire, Peter Wheeler, and John O'Driscoll to score the Lions' try in the First Test. Morne du Plessis, the Springbok captain with his eye half-closed, tries in vain to stop them.

ABOVE Clive Woodward licks his lips as he cuts past Naas Botha in the Second Test at Bloemfontein.

RIGHT South Africa's 'man of the series', Gysie Pienaar, the fullback holds the ball aloft in triumph after scoring the try in the Second Test which meant that South Africa could not lose the series. The dejected British Lion is Bruce Hay.

Angry faces in the Second Test: Bill Beaumont, the Lions captain, lies pointing a warning finger, while just over him is the scowling Louis Moolman. At the top Richard Prentis, then Maurice Colclough, and Martiens Le Roux watch expectantly as the ball is passed out. BELOW Bruce Hay makes sure of his try in the Third Test at Port Elizabeth.

The Lions come to town. Noel Murphy, escorted by one of the 'lovelies' on the pillion, rides in the parade as the cavalcade arrives in Pretoria for the match against Northern Transvaal. BELOW The hand of a hidden coloured player covers Peter Morgan's mouth as Phil Orr and Ian Stephens come to his rescue in the match against the South African Barbarians in Durban.

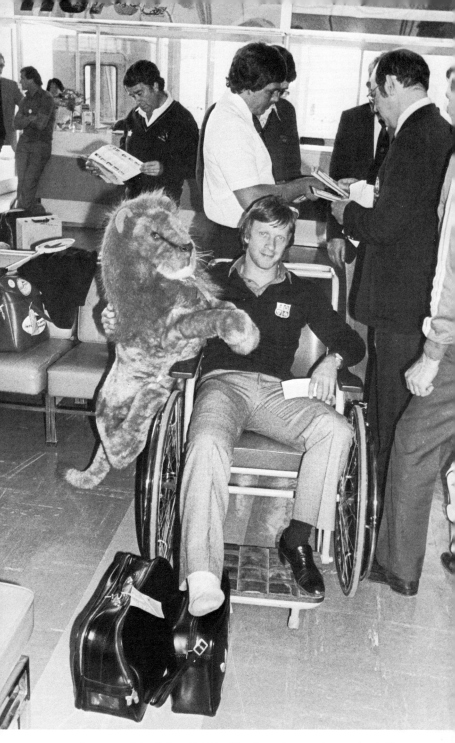

Just one of the Injured Pride. The Lions' mascot consoles Colin
Patterson at Kimberley on the way to Johannesburg.

ABOVE John O'Driscoll *(right)* sees his chance in the last Test at Pretoria. The ball lies handy, he seizes it, and, BELOW, charges over for a try.

At Last! *Victory.* Bill Beaumont wearing the laurel wreath of triumph is carried from the field after the last Test had been won by the Lions.

22
The Finishing Flourish

Few people outside the Lions' camp thought they had much chance of winning the fourth and final Test in Pretoria. No other Lions' team had done it in South Africa; even the highly successful 1974 side could only draw the last match of the series after winning the first three. Of the other major touring sides to visit South Africa, New Zealand had won the fourth Test on their 1928 tour, and in 1933 Australia won the fifth Test in a five-match series. The usual reasons advanced for the extreme difficulty of winning this last game are that the visiting players' thoughts are turned towards home, that they are occupied with buying presents, saying 'Good-bye' to the large numbers of new friends they have made, and generally preparing for the journey home. They have little time to think of Rugby Football. Dr Danie Craven said quite frankly that it was wrong to end a tour with an international match. Yet it has always been done, and probably always will be, for the event must finish with a climax. One or two minor matches after the last Test would be useless.

However, inside the Lions' camp, in spite of all the distractions, far from there being a despondent mood as to the outcome of the game, there was an air of determination, a resolution that there should be no 'whitewash'. It was quite amazing how the general state of mind of the individuals in the party, which for want of a better word we call 'team spirit', remained buoyant to the end in spite of every setback. Maybe that was one of the reasons why these Lions were such popular tourists. They had suffered many bitter blows and disappointments, and perhaps they knew in their silent thoughtful moments that they might inadvertently commit again some of those Rugby sins that had beset them. Yet they refused to show it, and they went into the game with a confident air.

Perhaps it was their confidence and determination, more than anything else, that enabled them to achieve the seemingly impossible; particularly the determination of the forwards, for there were times during the match when the old troubles of the backs returned. They beat South Africa 17–13, showing at last what could and should have been done in the other Tests. However it is of little use to reflect afterwards on what might have been; we must deal with facts.

The splendid Loftus Stadium in Pretoria was packed with a capacity crowd of sixty-eight thousand, all seated. There had been a tremendous scramble for tickets, and for the first time on the tour the touts had done a roaring trade. All South Africa wanted to be there to see, as they anticipated, the Springboks achieve the series grand slam in the sunshine of Pretoria. For their captain, Morne du Plessis, such an outcome on this ground was essential to obliterate his memory of the match played there six years earlier. On that occasion he had been in the Springbok side who had lost to the Lions by a record margin, and he had been dropped for the remainder of the series. A final victory here would have erased that memory, but it was not to be.

If ever a pack of forwards was completely outplayed and mastered in an international match, it was the pack in which Morne du Plessis was captain that day. The Lions won overwhelming possession, and for most of the game had the Springboks in constant retreat. By half-time they ought to have held such a commanding lead that the South Africans could not possibly have caught them. In fact they led by four points. There had been a few moments here and there when it seemed that the Lions were back in the old rut. Ollie Campbell's goal-kicking, for instance, was erratic again. In the home championship he had hardly ever missed; in the Tests in South Africa his performance was quite the reverse. He missed with important kicks at Bloemfontein, at Port Elizabeth, and again at Loftus Versfeld, where in the whole match he succeeded with only two kicks from eight attempts. Late in the game Andy Irvine ignored an overlap and a try was lost, but this time there was compensation for these errors.

Campbell may have been off target with the boot, but his running was much more effective, and he played an important part in the Lions' first try. Irvine began the move in his own half, fastening on to a poor kick and giving Campbell the chance to show himself as an elusive runner. John O'Driscoll, the outstanding player in a magnificent pack, was up with Campbell and drove on twenty-five metres, tantalizingly near the Springboks' line. Van Heerden stopped him, but O'Driscoll made sure the ball was available for Clive Williams, who was shoved over by his fellow forwards for the try. By then Campbell had missed four penalty kicks, so Irvine was called upon to make the conversion attempt, and he also missed. So Campbell and Botha each having kicked a penalty goal earlier, the Lions led by 7–3.

The Springboks had hardly been in the game, but as before they were quite capable of hanging on in the hope that eventually the Lions would give enough away to be beaten. It was a coincidence, and perhaps ominous, that the Lions had also led 7–3 at Port Elizabeth. On that occasion the Springboks had followed up by scoring three times. This time it became frighteningly apparent that they might do the same thing again. Botha set up a try for them, picking up a loose ball and making a lot of ground before passing to Willie du Plessis who swerved past a couple of Lions with tantalizing ease and touched down near the posts. Botha's conversion attempt hardly got off the ground. At this point, though, the Springboks enjoyed their one period of domination. Botha had been jeered by the crowd for his kicking failures, and Gysie Pienaar was given the kick from fifty-two metres when the Lions got off-side. With all the confidence of a man at his peak, he kicked a beautiful goal. Two minutes later the Lions again were off-side and again Pienaar, from a much narrower angle, kicked the penalty goal. It was not the first time in the series that the Springboks had been able to look at the scoreboard and wonder why they were six points up in a match that ought to have spelt for them comprehensive defeat.

The Lions' forwards, however, fought back as they had so often done before, and for a short time that determination with which they had gone into the match became apparent not only in the pack but among the backs as well. While the forwards maintained complete and utter control, the backs, perhaps out of embarrassment, began to move the ball with some resolution. They handled it out to Bruce Hay on the left wing – not at a great pace – but Irvine got up in support, and when Hay was tackled Irvine gathered the ball quickly and got over in the corner. There was a suspicion that Irvine was off-side, but the referee was up with the play and saw nothing wrong. After a moment's hesitation he awarded the try which gave Irvine the four points he needed to equal the world record of 210 set by Phil Bennett in thirty-seven internationals. Irvine had played in forty-six.

The try which won the match came soon afterwards when Irvine, having failed to give John Carleton the ball with the Springbok line wide open, was ankle-tapped by Pienaar. The Lions recaptured the ball, Tucker and Squire rolled it, O'Driscoll supported, and with several Springboks on his back scored the try so close in that Campbell could not possibly miss the conversion.

There were a few minutes still to go, but the Lions had their tails up by then and maintained command, while John Robbie kept the ball tight. At last the Lions had won! Certainly they deserved to do so this time. They had destroyed the Springbok pack, and even the experienced Morne du Plessis was near to panic. Only Willie du Plessis and Pienaar behind the scrum played with anything like the skill expected at the top level. Had there been a fifth Test the South African selectors must have made changes, because they could not have returned to the fray with that side. For the first time in the series their mediocrity had been thoroughly exposed by the Lions, whose forwards had never played better. Syd Millar said he had never seen a better pack, which was praise indeed for he had coached the 1974 forwards to a new peak of efficiency.

Tobias Steals Show
by Carwyn James

The Lions had shown exceptional determination in their build-up to the last Test. Against the Barbarians at Durban their superior team-work and drill had paid the right kind of dividend. This time they again displayed their team-work and efficiency, but still the most memorable moments of the day came from Hugo Porta, Errol Tobias and Mark Loane. Tobias and Loane played for the Junior Springboks against the Barbarians in the curtain-raiser before the Test. A packed house had gathered early because there was a feeling that the curtain-raiser would be the better spectacle and the Test an anti-climax. That was not the case, though. The Springbok forwards, led by Loane, were much too good for the loose play of the Ba-Baas' forwards, and even Jean-Pierre Rives, one of the outstanding flankers of the seventies, could not raise his game. Behind a beaten pack Hugo Porta again looked the class player that he is, but long before the end even he had to show the white flag. In fact Tobias stole the show. He played so well at outside-half that I honestly think that had he displayed that form in an earlier match we might have seen the first black player in the Springbok team for the last Test. This was the private dream of Danie Craven, and it would have borne out Butch Lochner's prediction that the series would probably produce the first non-white wearing of a Springbok jersey.

With the curtain-raiser over, and an overwhelming victory won by the Junior Springboks, we sat back and wondered how the Lions would fare in the final fling of a tough tour. The odds were against them, yet Beaumont's boys knew that only ill luck or fate had robbed them of victory at Port Elizabeth. Since that stormy day they had easily disposed of the Barbarians, Western Province had been even easier, and the mid-week XV had eventually tamed the ferocious forward effort of the Griquas. Preserving their unbeaten record against the provincial and six other scratch sides had given the Lions the uplift they needed, and that combined with their deep sense of hurt following the previous Test gave them just the motivation they needed. Their opponents had nothing to fight for except to outdo the Lions of 1974, who had inflicted the greatest indignity ever on a nation proud of its Rugby history.

Sitting there with Chris Rea preparing for the last radio commentary, I could not help recalling what the Lions had really achieved, despite the euphoria with which they approached their last confrontation with the Springboks. They had scored three tries in each of their last two matches, admittedly, but at Cape Town they had scored the first from an interception, the second from a forward pass, and the third was made possible by two loose scrums and a little bit of luxury in the passing between Campbell, Dodge and Woodward. At Kimberley Stephens fed the ball back from a maul for Beattie to score, Robbie was fed from a five-yard scrum to score the second, and Morgan got the last when Woodward pounced on a Griquas handling error. Not a single try came from a well-executed threequarter passing movement.

At the final whistle of the last Test I felt a deep sense of relief because the Lions had survived after once again showing an infinite capacity to destroy themselves. Somehow they had seemed to defy the age-long principles of the game, including the basic one that the side which wins the most possession should win. With the amount of the ball they won in the first half they should have led by five times the four-point margin which the scoreboard showed. The pack, hunting together with power and pride, were yards too quick for their opponents, and with so much pressure inflicted on Morne's men the tries surely ought to have come. Yet in that glorious first half of power play they scored only one try, initiated by their backs and finished off by Clive Williams, who was the epitome of the saying that props should never be seen.

At half-time I had the uneasy feeling that I had seen this many times before: power play resulting in little actual reward, and the inevitable boost it gives to the opposition, who know that if they can stem attack upon attack, then surely, most surely, their moment will come. And it came. Botha did the approach work, and Willie du Plessis finished off the movement with a brilliant piece of running. Pienaar, unquestionably the man of the series, did the kicking that mattered, and the Lions were six points adrift – two knock-out punches, and both beautifully timed.

While the Lions' fight-back earned them eternal credit, even when Irvine scored -- if he did – the passing was still shoddy, and it was a near miracle that the ball got that far. Then Irvine had the Springboks, their line, and the silent crowd at his mercy, but he stuttered and fell, and failed to pass to Carleton. Irvine, more than anyone, I am sure, must have been relieved when O'Driscoll scored the all-important try for his team to win the match. O'Driscoll, I thought, was the most improved player in the Lions' squad.

There is no doubt that the Lions deserved their victory; a victory which only underlined the fact that they were the better side in the series but applied their talents to mediocre effect.

23
The Colours
Unite

After all the excitement, with the matches all played and the journeying finished, we had time to think, and to recall what we had seen and heard in that troubled yet still remarkable country. Near the end of the tour it had been announced that by the following year the South African Rugby Board, the South African Rugby Football Federation and the South African Rugby Association, representing, respectively, the white players, the coloured players and the black players, would all be brought together under the same umbrella. That would be an immense step forward towards the integration of the races in Rugby Football. It was a pity that the South African Rugby Union, which also represents black players, would have nothing to do with the other organizations. Dick Jeeps, as chairman of the British Sports Council, said at the time that he thought the South African Rugby Board should make peace with the Union. How soon that might come about, if ever, no one can tell, but it certainly would be pleasing to British eyes if all four organizations were amalgamated.

Still, the uniting of the three was a fine thing for the British in South Africa to contemplate, because, to tell the truth, most of us were a little disappointed at the slow progress made towards integration. It is true that England had played a Federation side and a Bantu side on their tour of South Africa in 1972, and on this Lions tour for the first time a multi-racial side had faced them. When the Lions played these mixed sides there was complete integration afterwards. They could all drink in the same bar, and at every match the races were mixed in the stands. The corrals for the coloureds stood only as relics of the past. The mixture did not appear to go very deep, however. While the spectators were thoroughly integrated, the game itself was not. Although the machinery exists for black and coloured players to join and play for clubs which have hitherto been exclusively for whites, very few blacks and coloureds are to be found in these clubs. The only truly multi-racial club is a military one called the Defence Club in Cape Town. They provided the opposition for the Springboks prior to the first Test in Cape Town. The sight of the black wing Nicki Davids taking part in a Springbok practice was evidence that some progress had been made, but the playing standards of the blacks and coloureds was generally poor; indeed it appeared to have deteriorated. Only one or two black or coloured players were anywhere near top level. Errol Tobias, for instance, the coloured outside-half who had played against England in 1972 and had been in the South African Barbarian side in Britain in 1979, played in the Boland side, but he and Hennie Shields, another coloured player who was reckoned at one time to have a chance of getting into the Springbok side, were outstanding exceptions. We surmised that the reason for so few non-whites reaching the top was the lack of coaching of the youngsters. The changes that had been made in Rugby had not got down to the grass roots. Perhaps under the new regime in Rugby that will be remedied.

Dr Craven claimed that Rugby Football had shown other sports, and indeed the domestic life of the nation, the way towards integration of the races. Perhaps he was right, but the facts that we found were that both cricket and athletics had overtaken Rugby. Cricket had gone gaily ahead simply by ignoring the laws which banned blacks and coloureds in certain areas, and the law relating to the consumption of alcohol in certain premises, as it applied to drinking in clubs. Rugby, perhaps because in South Africa it is not so much a sport as the nation's way of life, and therefore closer to the government, had been more circumspect. Dr Craven had obviously done a tremendous amount – everything he possibly could – to work towards the desired goal, but his hands were often tied by those who held political power. He claimed that Rugby had gone a long way in the last ten years by following a set programme in which they started at the top. In fact amalgamation at the top had only just come about. In the next ten years they will have to work downwards to the grass roots which are so important.

The Rugby rulers of all races in South Africa recognize the difficulty of integration in a country where the basis of the law is disintegration. However, as Mr Chernish Mdyesha the President of SARA said, sport, and particularly Rugby, could give the necessary lead to bring about changes in the social system of the country.

They should go as far as they could within the limits of the present social state, and not turn back just because the laws of the country were at the moment against them. 'You can hear white schoolchildren at matches shouting for SARA,' he said. 'Such integration is bound to have an effect on society in the long run.'

Whether the fact that the Lions made their tour to South Africa helped the move towards integration is open to argument. Our opinion is that it may not have done much good in that direction, but it certainly did no harm. The announcement about the amalgamation of three of the ruling bodies in South Africa was well timed, but really had not much to do with the Lions' visit. The organizations had obviously been discussing the subject for a long time. However, Dr Craven thought the tour had done a great deal of good. 'It has revived many of our needs,' he told us. 'One is the reunion of people all over the country. They meet at Test matches, and they have their fun because they are away from their normal environment and their ordinary routine. They forget themselves. People in South Africa are united because they have a touring side to enjoy. Changes have taken place in our game, and we can now see what such changes could do to the whole country, and how the whole country could reap the benefits.'

Mr Mydesha was perhaps not quite so enthusiastic when we asked him about the Lions' tour. He said it had shown that the progress that had been made in South Africa was small, but added philosophically, 'Any progress at all is progress.' His counterpart in the coloured organization, Mr Cuthbert Loriston, told us that at first he had had his reservations about the wisdom of making the tour, especially in view of the Gleneagles agreement. He thought it would be embarrassing 'our friends' to ask them to make the tour, but now he was prepared to say that any good that could be achieved by a tour would be achieved by this one. He added, 'One thing we will find is that we have more money for projects which we have in mind, because we hope we will be able to share in the profits of the tour.' He should be well satisfied on that point. Estimates of the profits ranged up to well over two million pounds.

Syd Millar, perhaps naturally, displayed much more optimism about the results of the tour. 'Certainly it has been a success,' he said. 'We have not won the Test series, but there is much more to a tour than that. I think we were right to come. The Four Home Unions, I am sure, knew that everything was not right in South Africa, but they knew people were trying to change the old ways, and a tour could encourage that. I think it was in recognition of the work Dr Craven and the leaders of the black and coloured organizations had done that we came. Anyone coming to South Africa for the first time would not know what changes had taken place, but my visits have spanned a long time, and the changes are very apparent to me, and some of them are radical. Of course Rugby Football cannot change the law of the land, but it can bring the advantage of making changes to people's minds, and in the end will bear fruit.

'We are the first Lions' side to play against mixed teams, and that is progress. Noel Murphy had not been to South Africa since 1961, and as we stood together on a platform before the speeches at one of the functions and looked down the hall we saw so many non-white faces. Noel thought it was absolutely amazing. To people who know South Africa that is very significant. These are changes that bring everyone on to common ground, and don't forget Rugby is a good method of communication. We must not lose sight of the objects of the tour. While to the average South African I suppose the Test matches are the main objective, I think the aim should go farther than that to see if it is possible for Springbok sides to tour overseas. That would be a good idea, because just as our Lions' players will be interviewed by the Press and on television when they go home, so would the Springboks be questioned when they returned home to South Africa from an overseas tour. They could then make a few points to many millions of people. It would be a way of opening people's minds. You see you cannot play any game in a team with fellows of another race without getting to know them pretty well. You'll find that if you can work together in sport you can work together in a lot of other areas. It's a slow process, but it is progress.'

Millar went on to say that the players went to South Africa first of all because they wanted to become Lions, and they had open minds when they arrived as to what they were going to find. They knew that changes had taken place in South African Rugby, and that many of the objections had disappeared – not all of them, but many. Those who had been to South Africa before, such as himself, were impressed, even though the changes did not appear to be great. The players who were there for the first time may not have been happy about certain things, but one could go to any country in the world and not be happy about some of the things they did. The players, he said, had looked outside the Rugby atmosphere, and certainly apartheid was something they just could not accept. They also realized that such a situation could not be changed overnight. The Press sometimes pointed out the bad things without emphasizing the good things, and there had been many good things for the players. They had been happy to be there as Rugby players; they appreciated the country; they had reservations about it, but he would be very surprised if many of them said they did not want to return to South Africa. He added that he was going to recommend that the Lions should tour there again; that was, unless the situation changed very much for the worse.

So far as Rugby is concerned, it appeared to us that the situation would change for the better. Dr Craven told us that from the next year onwards they would start to get right down to the grass roots. The South African Rugby Board would be the supreme body responsible for the sport, and the government would recognize that. They would be responsible for players of all races, both financially and in the matter of facilities for playing. 'It is a big thing that is happening next year,' he said.

Bill Beaumont was convinced that the tour had helped the black and coloured players. 'We have played against more multi-racial sides than any other tourists,' he said, 'and if nothing else that has helped the situation in South Africa for the Rugby players. We came to help them, and I have absolutely no regrets about coming on this trip. It does not mean that we support what is going on in South Africa, and in fact I think we are helping to make progress just by talking to people and letting our views be known.'

His summing up of the actual play was predictable. Apart from the abnormal number of injuries, he thought they had lost the Test series principally because they did not take their chances. Injuries had meant that they had had to play ten different half-back pairings in almost the same number of matches, and so they had not been able to develop a good combination and the players had not been confident. They had missed to a very great extent players like Terry Holmes, Gareth Davies, Dai Richards and Mike Slemen.

He agreed that perhaps they had put too much emphasis on forward play, but he pointed out that all the great sides in the past had done that. The 1974 Lions in South Africa were based totally on forwards, and they dominated the series through their pack. But, he went on, they also had Gareth Edwards and Phil Bennett at their peak. The inference was obvious when he pointed out that Peter Wheeler, Jeff Squire, Graham Price and he had played in five consecutive Tests for the Lions (two in New Zealand and, up to that time, three in South Africa) and had dominated the forward play, yet still had lost.

After we had had this chat, Beaumont led his side to victory in the last Test, so perhaps there are still some good British backs, if not as many as there were in 1971 in New Zealand. Beaumont said he still felt that, as in New Zealand in 1977, they had created enough chances to have won the games, but the backs had suffered through lack of confidence in each other. With players like Ollie Campbell, Paul Dodge and Mike Slemen, not to mention others like Steve Fenwick who were unavailable, he thought the British Isles still had some outstanding backs. What exasperated him was that the Springbok backs were poor, except for Pienaar. If he had not been playing the Springboks would have been in a lot of trouble.

Even Dr Craven agreed that the general standard of South African play was poor. He thought their period of isolation in the 1970s had caused them to fall off considerably. They had started playing pattern Rugby, and that really killed the game because it stifled individualism. Pattern Rugby was caused by over-coaching. It was bad for the game if the coach moulded the individual into a form which he wanted and not one which suited the individual. The best coaching one could get was to watch others. 'I used to travel a very long way to see a scrum-half who played for South Africa,' he said. 'The best coaching is through the eyes.'

His final words can be echoed throughout the Rugby-playing world. 'My one wish now', he said 'is that the youth of South Africa shall have the same opportunity that I had, to be welcome to play anywhere in the world and without any side issues.'

24
The Press Gang

Not only did the 1980 Lions have to cope with an unprecedented number of injuries, but they had following them the largest Press gathering ever to attach itself to a Rugby tour. Allowing for regional variations there were about fifty writers, broadcasters and photographers accompanying the party. For the first week at least that meant about two media men to each player.

By the end of the tour, with replacements having arrived at the rate of about one a week, the players were catching up fast. The political significance of the tour added to its attraction for the world's Press, and one or two of the writers spent more of their time in the towns than they did on the Rugby fields. It is naive to imagine that sport and politics can be kept separate in these times, but throughout the tour articles appeared on the sports pages of some newspapers which would have been better suited to the political sections. While respecting the judgement of sports editors and news editors, we sometimes thought that this was an extra pressure with which the players had to contend. During the last week of the tour Syd Millar highlighted this additional burden in an interview with an Afrikaans journalist, John du Toit, who quoted him as saying that because of articles written in the British Press about the political side of the tour, the wives and families of one or two players had been threatened and harrassed. The majority of the Pressmen on the tour thought that, not for the first time, they were being held responsible for the actions of a minority. So, in the foyer of the Kimberley hotel, the majority made their thoughts very clear to Millar. In fairness to Millar it must be recorded that in the interview with du Toit he had merely responded to a question about the differences between touring South Africa and touring New Zealand and Australia. Naturally enough some of the differences were political, and he had given examples to make his point.

There were times when the Press and the officials of various Rugby organizations did not see eye to eye, which is understandable, but Dr Craven's harangue after the first Test, and 'Butch' Lochner's statement before the second Test, which brought to a sudden end the dialogue between the Press and the Springbok management, were more than just unfortunate. So was the statement by one journalist that fifty per cent of the Lions were unhappy and wanted to go home. He claimed that he had been misquoted, and perhaps he had, but when a player challenged him to name one Lion who wanted to leave he was unable to do so.

The very size of the Press party limited the opportunities for them to relax with the players. Usually it is possible on tour to arrange some sort of competition, either on the squash court or the golf course. In New Zealand in 1977, a tour that was not renowned for good relations between players and Press, several joint excursions were organized. That did not happen this time, and in fact so constant was the presence of the Press around the players, that the players could not be begrudged their privacy during their hours of relaxation. So the Press made their own arrangements, which began with the early morning jog for those who were determined to keep fit, to get fit or to commit suicide. Fortunately there were no fatalities, but the numbers dwindled from the enthusiastic dozen who started during the first week at Vanderbijlpark to the three hardy souls who completed the course ten weeks later at Pretoria. By then the jog had matured into a reasonably competitive run lasting about thirty-five minutes and covering roughly five miles.

The coach was Ian Todd, of The *Sun*, who had previously run in the New York marathon, and was preparing himself to run in it again. From the start he was in good physical shape, which was more than could be said for some of the others. Todd took the greatest care of his team, however, falling back every now and then to offer words of encouragement to those for whom the pain barrier was proving insurmountable. There were casualties which reduced the number as the tour progressed. The flu bug which went around sometimes came as a welcome relief to the reluctant jogger, sparing him the agony of the 7.30 a.m. call and the threatened fine for non-attendance. There were sprained ankles, torn ligaments, and Todd himself awoke one morning with the dreaded pain which affects so many athletes. His knee was inflamed and clicked ominously. The cartilage would have to come out, and so Todd, like many of the players, made his way to Clive Noble's clinic in Johannesburg for advice and treatment. Noble had done magnificent work for the Lions; without him their injury problems would have been much greater. The management had enormous faith in his ability, and quite rightly so. When Colin Patterson was so badly injured at Kimberley, it was decided to postpone the operation on his knee ligaments for twenty-four hours in order that it could be done by Noble, who was due to begin his holidays that day. Noble had decided that his holidays could wait, and set about the task of sewing Patterson's severed ligaments together, an operation which lasted two hours.

Todd's operation was simple by comparison, and one which Noble had perfected. Within twenty-four hours the patient was covering a Rugby match, and within four days he was back on the jogging circuit.

Considering the size of the Press party, relationships among the scribes remained remarkably free of rancour. For the visiting journalists it was a revelation to see how much copy their South African counterparts were required to produce each day. Often one journalist would contribute five or six articles to the same edition, which seemed a ludicrous work-load and an inevitable drain on his talent. Perhaps it was the strain of turning out so much material that told on Mike Shafto of the *Evening Star*. He never ran out of words, but he ran out of jackets, absent-mindedly leaving one in each of the hotels between East London and Windhoek.

At nearly every stop the Press stayed in the same hotel as the team, which was sometimes as annoying for the Press as it was for the players. Mostly the standard of hotels was high, but because of a deal negotiated by the South African Rugby Board some of the hotels were sub-standard. In view of the profits made by the tour, one would have thought it would be the aim of the host country to ensure that the touring side was given the best possible accommodation. Fruit machines in the foyer, lunchtime strip shows in the bar, and piped music everywhere may be considered by some people to be the last word in luxury, but they do not tend to make for the most relaxed atmosphere. On the night before one of the Tests there was such a rumpus in the hotel, with fist fights and hooting of horns, that the team could not sleep. The fact is that the better the hotel, the less likelihood there is of such disturbances.

However variable the standard of the hotels, their quality was higher than some of the grounds selected for the Tests. The exception was Loftus Versfeld at Pretoria. This is one of the best appointed grounds in the world, but neither Newlands at Cape Town nor Boet Erasmus at Port Elizabeth was suitable for housing a match of such importance. Bill Beaumont described the Newlands pitch as a 'cabbage patch', and to a self-respecting cabbage patch that might have been insulting. The excuse was made that the bare areas along the touchlines were caused by the stand preventing the sun from reaching them. That, however, is a problem which the ground staff at Twickenham seem to overcome every year. It was also said that the advice of experts from all over the world had been sought, and that every known variety of grass had been tried without success. While it may be true that the problem was caused partly by lack of sun and difficulties with the soil, it could hardly have been helped by the number of matches played on the ground. There were at least three games a week on the pitch for two months before the Lions' visit, and some had been played when the ground was water-logged. Surely, in view of the Lions' visit, it would have been wise to restrict the number of games at Newlands? The accommodation for spectators had been greatly improved with the building of a new stand, the railway stand, but a ground so famous and so impressive in its situation deserves a better playing surface.

Boet Erasmus was the other sea-level venue for the Tests, and that by British standards was unsafe. The day before the third Test a woman fell between the struts in the scaffolding stand and broke her leg. On the day of the match the weather was so bad that many thousands stayed at home and watched the game on television, so the ground was nothing like full. With a capacity crowd we could imagine that the problems of crowd control would be almost insuperable. The pitch, with its blue Kentucky grass, was first-class, but the situation of it was such that the angle of the afternoon sun made watching the ball very difficult for the players facing it in the second half.

Because of massive reconstruction work at Ellis Park, Johannesburg, the Tests at altitude were played at Bloemfontein and Pretoria. The Ellis Park development is unique, and when it is complete this will surely be the finest Rugby stadium in the world. There will be hospitality suites, restaurants, a completely relaid pitch and play-back facilities on a giant screen. The criticism of Boet Erasmus applied equally to the stadium at Bloemfontein. The stands were hazardous, crowd control difficult, and as with all pitches encircled by a running track, the viewing positions were unsatisfactory. So Loftus Versfeld was at the time of our visit the best appointed ground in South Africa, although King's Park in Durban had an attractive traditional charm all of its own.

25
Grand
Summing-Up
by Carwyn James

The Lions could and should have won the series. At no time, from the first Test to the fourth, did I feel that the task of beating the Springboks was beyond them. The opposition never reached a very high standard, and certainly not the heights of the Springboks of the fifties and sixties. Measured by such a golden yardstick, 1980 was not a vintage year. The Rugby played lacked the power and steel which normally makes Test matches between the major countries something special. The series was a Test series in name only. The tries scored – and there were a dozen in the first two internationals – came mostly through errors made by players who wilted under pressure. Creative movements, even of average quality, were as scarce as Kimberley rain.

Isolated, South Africa had suffered. Starved of Test match experience and overseas tours, their players were content with the introverted, self-imposed standards of the Currie Cup. Competitions laid too much stress on winning, and the powers who controlled the game seemed to have decided that if kicking goals was the key to success, then they would play the kicking game. It was not unusual for Northern Transvaal to win a match simply by deft use of the boot, scoring upwards of forty points but not a single try.

Having been bored to tears by the pathetic, uncoordinated back play of Naas Botha's Northern Transvaal team, I felt it was my duty to the game to tell some thirty of that Province's qualified coaches that the basic skills of passing and handling had been badly taught to their top players. There were nods of approval, intelligent questioning, but while the likes of Botha reign supreme with their boots, the approach will always be wrong. Winning becomes more important than the manner of winning. Before taking a coaching session at Windhoek High School for sixteen-year-olds and under, I talked to them at length about the approach to the game, emphasizing over and over again that Rugby is a running and a handling game, and that they should emulate a Gavin Cowley and not a Naas Botha. I qualified my remarks about the *young* Naas Botha who, four years earlier, had impressed the 1976 All Blacks, and whom J.J. Stewart, the coach, regarded as a better player than Gerald Bosch, the Springboks' outside-half. Botha then had yet to start worrying about winning matches at any price.

I mentioned to the lads of Windhoek that at the start of one season at Llandovery College, in the pre-dispensation law period, I insisted that no player should ever kick the ball in any of their matches. It was one of the finest seasons we ever had. I then asked the Windhoek boys to play a practice match before I took the coaching session. The headmaster was amazed, and a little thrilled, that not a single boy kicked the ball in thirty minutes, not even the lad who had confided that he wanted to be a Naas Botha.

This emphasis on winning at all costs has had a sad effect in other ways too. During the dry, hot winter of 1980 in South Africa, ideal for training and for playing, I saw too little joy and contentment on the faces of young men playing their chosen game. I saw stress and strain, haste and hurry, courage and conviction, but little that was leisurely and unhurried. There was a lack of class, and with one or two exceptions, Mike Slemen and Gareth Davies for instance, there was a lack of star quality. The presence of Hugo Porta on the field, and Barry John and Phil Bennett in the stand in the later stages of the tour, reminded us of the higher standards and the keener pleasure we should be able to expect from Test Rugby.

Perhaps it is easier to maintain standards in a game like cricket, which is dominated by the individual. Some of the best cricketers in the world in the seventies were South Africans, and the famous radio commentator, Charles Fortune, now the secretary of the multi-racial South African Cricket Board, told us over dinner one evening at the magnificent Wanderers Club in Johannesburg, that tremendous interest is generated every summer in their Cup competitions because of the presence of real star quality. (As I write, on my return from the tour, I notice that Peter Kirsten, who played well at outside-half for the Quaggas-Barbarians combination against the 1974 Lions, kicking four penalties, and Allan Lamb, another South African, head the batting averages in our own County Championship.)

There is some excuse for a deterioration in standards in a country suffering from isolation. There is little excuse for a worse deterioration in British Rugby.

Most members of the Four Home Unions Tours Committee, our representatives on the International Board and the Presidents of the Home Unions spent a few weeks observing the tour as guests of the South African Rugby Board. The French contingent, headed by Albert Ferrasse, who arrived for the last Test, were guests of the South African Government. The Chairman of the Committee, Mickey Steele-Bodger, was in attendance at the third and fourth Tests. Even before he received a detailed report on the tour from Messrs Millar and Murphy, he could profitably have called a meeting to discuss one simple, honest question: 'Where did we go wrong?'

Leaving aside the question of tactics, to which I shall return, it seems to me that they were wrong from the beginning in not selecting the management early in 1979. Interviews for the posts are usually held in May of the year preceding the tour, and by the first week of June a manager, an assistant manager and a coach have been appointed. This allows them the summer and a full season in which to prepare.

This effective system was established by John Tallent, an exceptionally far-seeing chairman of the Committee. It was he, together with its secretary, John Hart, now the secretary of the International Board, who laid the foundations for the successes of 1971 and 1974. They were driven to make this move by the bitter experience of the 1966 tour of Australia and New Zealand, which had presented shattering problems for the coach, John

Robins, the captain, Mike Campbell-Lamerton, and the manager, Des O'Brien – problems which they never resolved. By the time the Lions left for South Africa in 1968, however, David Brooks, Ronnie Dawson and Tom Kiernan had been given every opportunity to make their preparations, and since that year the procedure formulated by Tallent had been used for every tour.

While I sympathize with Steele-Bodger and his Committee, I feel very strongly that they made a serious mistake by not selecting their management at the right time, whether they thought the tour was on or not. As it was, when the world's attention was turned away from South African politics and on to the Soviet invasion of Afghanistan, and hence the Olympics, and the decision was finally made that the tour could go ahead, the Committee were hurried into last-minute decisions in the new year. Syd Millar and Noel Murphy, worthy men and worthy choices, were faced with an extremely difficult task. Time, if nothing else, was against them.

The Management

No man was ever better qualified to manage a touring team in South Africa than the genial Syd Millar of Ballymena. A robust tourist himself with the Lions in 1962 and 1968, he returned to South Africa as a highly successful coach of the unbeaten Lions of 1974. In his witty, punchy speeches at the post-match receptions of the grog and buffet kind, Millar would often refer to himself as a dull donkey or an unintelligent prop. In his pleasant lilting voice he would tell stories against himself and against his people. Then, suddenly, he would be all seriousness: 'The important thing is that we are here.'

Millar knew his audiences well. He had a fine sense of occasion and timing, and knew precisely when to turn on his engaging smile, and when to call a spade a spade. When he felt that some straight talking was called for, he pulled no punches, and he never spared the Press. 'Listen for a change, and report the facts,' he said on one occasion.

Bill Beaumont, on the other hand, always seemed to be bright and bouncing, and showing his teeth in that familiar grin. He would nervously preface his speeches with the inevitable apology in the unaccustomed-as-I-am-to-public-speaking style before handing out the goodies to his opposite number, the referee and the touch-judges. Beaumont was as diplomatic as the Speaker of the House of Commons, considering that he had to make polite noises to some of the worst referees in the world.

He is a gentle, likeable person who grew in stature as a captain. Considering the political undertones, the long list of injuries, and the innumerable off-the-field duties he had to perform, I would rate him as one of the successful captains despite the loss of the series. On the field he played his heart out but never quite displayed the form he had shown three years earlier in New Zealand.

I had the impression that Beaumont got on with the Press better than his manager did. I am not surprised really, because in the unreal season leading up to the tour Fleet Street had made a cult hero of this likeable Lancastrian. Featured in the tabloids, wooed by women columnists, Beaumont, it could be said, owed his position largely to the power of the English Press.

Millar appeared to be a little wary of the Press as a body. This was understandable, I suppose, since there were so many journalists of different breeds and convictions, each greedy for his copy to meet morning and evening deadlines. I felt that Millar would have been well advised to have held daily Press conferences at the start of the day. As it was, the conferences, if they could be so called, were haphazard, too often a hasty huddle on the field during a training session. At times there seemed to be a dreadful lack of, or delay in, communication between Millar and John Lawrence, the secretary of the Four Home Unions Tours Committee, particularly on the question of replacements, a recurring source of copy for the scribes. Too often we learned from Dublin, London or Cardiff who would be travelling as a replacement and when, and then we of the media would inform the management. It was a most unsatisfactory state of affairs.

When Colin Patterson was carried off the field at Kimberley, I telephoned my match report to the BBC in Cardiff immediately after the match, and without consultation with anyone, I said that the management would most certainly insist on a cover for John Robbie for the final Test, and that I considered Brynmor Williams, as a former Lion, to be the likely replacement. The Sports Department at the BBC naturally pursued the story.

The team and some of the Press were staying at the Kimberley Hotel, and I was at the same hotel as some Rugby Union officials. I failed to get the complete story from our end, so in order to broadcast live to Wales early the following morning, I had to get the full story from Cardiff, which I regurgitated for the nation. At breakfast time the authorities denied that it was a true version. Brynmor Williams had, in fact, confirmed that he was not at home when John Lawrence telephoned him. When eventually Lawrence got in touch with him he was told that someone else had accepted the call, and so Steve Smith made history by becoming the only Lion who never took the field.

Millar was always considerate and extremely patient, I thought, in dealing with irrelevant and inconsequential questions, and particularly so with one of the South African Press men who had a genius for asking the same question at least twice. On such occasions Millar's humour saved him, as it did, I am sure, with erring players.

If Millar was a disciplinarian he was a benign one. He was once described in my hearing as an enthusiastic poacher who had become a true and trusted gamekeeper, well versed in all the tricks of touring. He had grown out of having arguments with doors, he had amply tested the varying strengths of wine glasses, and he had learned his responsible lines by heart: 'There will be no violence, and no wrecking on this tour.' There was no real violence, and precious little wrecking.

Young in mind and in spirit, Millar was sympathetic with his players. I had the impression that he enjoyed the company of the young far more than that of the visiting Rugby Union alickadoos. In his assessment and selection of players he may have made the occasional mistake, but they were honest ones. Fair, considerate and sincere, Millar was a successful manager. Benefiting from his personal experience, he knew his place. Alun Thomas, the manager of the 1974 Lions, had given him his head as the coach, and Millar did for his team what he had already done for Ballymena and, more specifically, what Paul Roos, by telegram, had asked of the 1937 Springboks: 'Skrum, skrum, skrum.' Millar produced a most efficient scrum in 1974, the basis of a winning game from which Edwards and Bennett expertly profited at half-back, while J.P.R. was as safe as houses at full-back, and J.J. was a match-winning bonus.

I don't think any Lions coach would want to do the same onerous job twice. Millar was obviously content to let Noel Murphy get on with the playing side, but he was always at hand to discuss and encourage, and Murphy was sufficiently open-minded to use his manager's experience and expertise. It was perfectly natural that at some stage of the tour Millar would be called on to help with the scrummaging, and when Fran Cotton and Phil Blakeway had to call it a day, it was the moment for the manager to lend a hand. At the end of the first full coaching session in South Africa, Murphy, with a broad grin on his face, said to Millar and me that it was a little unfair to him that two former Lions' coaches should be there casting a critical eye on his performance. Point taken. Thereafter I maintained a 'low profile', but I kept in touch with the training sessions, which are so important for a professional critic who has to assess the qualities and the deficiencies of a team.

Murphy's sessions were always lively. The first few were too fierce, I thought. This was understandable, I suppose, because any coach wants to establish his authority over a new squad, but it is a temptation which must be resisted. Hay, Tomes and Quinnell, overweight and unfit, found the going hard. Murphy planned his sessions carefully, and he introduced plenty of variations to hold the interest of the players. His enthusiasm was infectious, and he was always appreciative of good work.

I found both manager and coach the most amenable of men, and I have every sympathy for the difficulties which Murphy had to endure throughout the tour. The injuries to key players, and there were too many, put him at a great disadvantage, and added to the stress. Even if he had wanted to play the extended game originally, I had the feeling that Millar, Murphy and Beaumont, all forwards, reverted to type fairly early on, thereby giving in to the notion that the backs could never develop into a winning combination. The winning, it must have been argued, was up front, and the ball, if relayed to the centre, had to be brought back to the forwards. So the positive Rugby succession of MacRae, Jansen and Gravell was nurtured.

It was at this point that I fundamentally disagreed, silently, with the policy and the tactics. I thought it unnecessary to turn the clock back to the days of MacRae, the predictable ploy of setting up the artificial platform for second-phase play. International players, if not already taught – and some of them were not – should at least be teachable. The once basic coaching requirement on this tour was the constant emphasis on moving the ball along the threequarter line at speed. In beautiful weather conditions, with a dry ball for every practice – except the one at Stellenbosch – the backs needed the discipline, under pressure, to take and give a pass in one stride. If it is not perfect you stop, and pass it again and again and again. These Lions went through the motions, but they were hardly ever stopped, and, like the Light Brigade, were never asked to reason why.

At the sight of anything short of perfect the coach should blow his whistle, but the play should continue. At or before the sound of the whistle the player taking the poor pass should take a second option, not the first option of relaying an indifferent transfer. If this basic, fundamental drill had been performed a thousand times a thousand during ten weeks of comparative neglect, we might have seen back play of international standard during the last month of the tour. As it was, these Lions were always at the primary whistle stage and, psychologically, because they showed no improvement, and did not realize why, most of them seemed to become more and more confused, and some of them were disheartened.

Even the most pedestrian of practitioners would have been capable of diagnosing the trouble at a glance, but an experienced consultant was needed to cure the differing ills of the various players. Murphy had played all his Rugby as a back-row man, a fast open-side flanker who destroyed outside-halves, and by the power of his tackling created attacking situations for his colleagues. Perhaps it was asking too much of a mortal who had spent a whole playing career destroying what was pleasing in mid-field play to emerge in later life as the creator of things bright and beautiful!

It would have been wrong even to suggest that Murphy should have surrendered his authority by asking for outside help. On my return I was informed, inaccurately, that 'Chalky' White, the Leicester coach, had been summoned to South Africa to help with the coaching of the backs. 'Chalky', in fact, was only there for the third Test to support the three men of Leicester, Wheeler, Dodge and Woodward. It is interesting to note, however, that when, following the defeat of the All Blacks in two of the three Tests in Australia, the New Zealand Rugby Council appointed Eric Watson of Otago as coach, they considered the principle of appointing an additional coach for the tour of Wales, Canada and the USA, to assist him with the backs. (Watson was a disciple of Victor Cavanagh who in the late 1940s perfected the ruck, and who died shortly after our return.)

Perhaps we are entering an era when two coaches will be appointed for a long tour. Not that I agree with the idea. Be that as it may, it must be said that while the Lions' forwards grew in stature as the tour progressed the backs did not improve, and may even have deteriorated. The irony of the situation was that Murphy had at hand a number of elder statesmen who could have helped to produce a formidable pack, but with the departure of Slemen there was no objective and experienced practitioner or analyst capable of teaching the backs.

The Tactics

Two years before the tour John Reason and I had written in this manner in *The World of Rugby*:

'Unfortunately, somewhere along the line, we seem to have lost the art of nurturing our backs. Law changes, in particular those relating to the off-side line, have given the mid-field players more time to think, and for the natural genius the thought process is less potent than the sudden instinctive impulse. The Bennetts of this world play far better in the open field from second phase possession or even from the non-quality ball which has 'Hospital' written all over it than they do from the quality possession, from the first phase set piece. In the modern game, probably because of the time and space factor, there are far too many pre-conceived ploys called by the pivot even before the ball has emerged from the set piece. The crash-ball ploys have become compulsive; the most pronounced, repetitive drill of the centre-cum-flanker type which we are breeding by the score. The variation has become the rule, and the rule, which has stood the test of time, the variation.'

So, it was an immense, perhaps even an impossible task which faced Murphy, the task of stemming the decline of British back play. Like a good man of Munster he found the practical considerations of the exercise far outweighed his sense of history, with the almost inevitable result that history will record that the decline continued. Within a minute of the first match played Murphy decided, with the loss of Stuart Lane, that he could not afford the ball to be moved too far away from the set piece. (Apocryphal or not, it is said of Ray Prosser, the coach of Pontypool, that he likes his scrum-half to play the game as an extra forward, that sometimes, but very occasionally, he can tolerate the outside-half having a touch of the ball, but if the ball is relayed any further it is a move, and 'Pross', it is said, does not like 'bloody moves'.)

The Lions embraced the one major move, and Ray Gravell,

overlooked for the first Test when the Lions were still unsure of their tactical game, became the hero – or the villain – of the crash-ball play. It might have been better to have experimented with a different kind of tactical ploy.

Outside-halves usually make exciting fullbacks. I have always been of the opinion that footballing flankers are capable of playing well in the centre, and I have no doubt that Steve Fenwick and Ray Gravell have the right instincts to be outstanding flankers. Rather than use Gravell constantly as a battering ram I would have experimented with a differing tactic by exploring the possibilities of using him in the centre, performing the basic role of the quick flanker. As a body the South African forwards were big and a shade ponderous. To render them less effective at the set pieces it was necessary to stretch them across the field as often as possible. This tactic would have been of considerable help to the Lions' pack.

To stretch the Springboks would mean moving the ball at speed along the threequarter line, and using Irvine outside the wing because of his greater pace and his experience of playing in that position. It is a fact of life in modern Rugby that the quick movement of the ball is facilitated by missing out one midfield player. Gravell would be the man to miss out so that he could loop around in support, and if the wing or Irvine was tackled in possession Gravell would be the first there by a mile to the point of breakdown. This would have offset any advantage gained by Rob Louw in other areas of play, while he, I am sure, would have found it a most frustrating experience to be beaten constantly to the wayward ball.

Another facet of play in which the Lions initially were startlingly inefficient was in defence. Ray McLoughlin always propounded the theory, with passion, that you should start building your team from back row defence. To concede ten tries in a couple of Test matches, as these Lions did, suggests weaknesses in their defensive organization and their tackling. No team likes operating in retreat. Accepting this fact, I have always been a great believer in asking players to run back twenty or thirty yards before going through the mechanics of mauling and rucking. I do not really see the point of always moving forward in practice sessions. The work-rate and the fitness attainment is at least halved. An added bonus of running back is the psychological gain of players getting used to retreat in order to attack, and in the process their defence – and this applies to the backs as well as to the forwards – gets better and better.

The Lions tightened their play a lot as the tour progressed. It is easy to say that they made too many elementary mistakes early on, but for every mistake there is a reason – a lack of technique, the wrong temperament under pressure, or a lapse of concentration. Each mistake has to be analysed. Coaching is not about units. The essence of coaching is the teaching of each and every individual. That is why clinics for the ailing individual are so important on tour. That is why a pool of consultants, capable diagnostics, can help the specialist who is expected to make all the right decisions.

All things considered, I must add that the backs were not always to blame. There were times when the Springboks' scrum was at least the equal of the Lions'. There were times when they were disrupted effectively by the use of the wheel. Moolman was easily the best exponent of the two-handed catch in both teams, and the Springboks read the rolling maul well, even though it was never developed by the Lions to more than about sixty per cent efficiency. What I am saying is that the ball the backs sometimes received was not relayed as quickly as it might, and it was not therefore of the right quality. To make matters worse, the Springbok backs in midfield were allowed by both Palmade and Bonnet to infringe the off-side law. I have innumerable mental pictures of Palmade's and Bonnet's backs as they studied the set pieces while the threequarters behind them were already taking advantage of the situation, and making life difficult for the poor midfield tourists.

History will record, incidentally, that for the first time in a major series there were neutral referees. South Africa and Dr Danie Craven can take the credit for this. Craven offered New Zealand neutral referees in 1976, which they refused, and ever

since the Kiwis have cursed their own Council and Gert Bezuidenhout of Transvaal, the referee in their third and fourth Tests,
who is about as unmentionable down under as Max Baise is to
the 1974 Lions. Craven was anxious to avoid that kind of
problem, and so for the visit of the Jaguars, the Welshman, Ken
Rowlands of Ynysybwl, was invited to referee the two Test
matches. Of the three invited referees the feeling in South Africa
was that Rowlands was far and away the best, Bonnet the
number two, and Palmade a very good number three.

I sincerely hope that the International Board will accept
neutral referees for all future major tours. South Africa is not
over-blessed with competent referees, so it is important that the
likes of Steve Strydom, the President of the Orange Free State,
and a member of the South African Rugby Board, get overseas
experience in France or in the UK, because there is little evidence
at the moment to suggest that either Australia or New Zealand
will accept the principle of neutrality.

It is an interesting fact that Steve Strydom, the best of the
South African referees, was apparently the man favoured by the
Board to act as liaison officer for Beaumont's Lions. Choot
Visser, the extremely popular liaison officer for the Lions in
1974, and a much less popular official with the All Blacks and
particularly with Noel Stanley, the manager, in 1976, was going
to be overlooked until Millar made a strong, personal request
for his services. Mr Visser again did a superb public relations
job, and he was extremely popular with the lads, and with the
British press, whom he entertained royally at his lovely home
in Bloemfontein. The centre-piece of his home is a Rugby
museum which is as magnificent as any in the world.

On the Sunday evening following the final Test hundreds of
people turned up at Jan Smuts Airport to say farewell to the
Lions, and Choot was not the only one who found it an
emotional occasion. Friendships, deep and lasting, are made on
these tours, and it is well to remember that, whatever the
political climate, much of their influence is undeniably for the
good.

South Africa's Rugby Future

Initially South Africa had been isolated because they rejected multi-racial sport. Basil D'Oliveira and the New Zealand Maoris, until the end of the sixties, were an embarrassment to the Nationalist Government. Gradually during the seventies multi-racial sport was introduced. Maoris became acceptable in 1970, and since then important strides had been made in soccer and cricket, while Rugby had lagged behind. Dr Craven, however, had worked really hard during the previous four years to get the support and the goodwill of the coloureds and the blacks.

In fairness to South Africa, the emphasis of their opponents had shifted from multi-racial sport to the whole question of apartheid. It was argued, and South Africa had to face the arguments, that it was not possible to be fully integrated in sport while the very laws of the land betrayed those same principles of integration. South Africa must make radical changes quickly. Time is not on the side of the white minority. They must, as soon as possible, legislate more in favour of their second-class citizens, educate them better, and give them far more responsibility in the running of the country. The voice of Bishop Desmond Tutu is an important one to which South Africa's Prime Minister must listen.

As I write Dr Craven and a number of officials and players have been refused visas to go to Argentina, so their projected tour to that country is probably off. New Zealand have delayed, yet again, their decision to invite the Springboks to their country next season. Ferrasse said that France might visit them in October, but by and large the isolation goes on. Teams visit South Africa, but the South Africans are not welcome overseas. It is a fact, and it has to be faced. The world simply does not accept apartheid. It just will not accept the fact that one colour of skin is better than another. Arguments about other 'isms', however evil, are irrelevant.

I sincerely hope that the South Africans themselves can solve this problem, peacefully, and without bloodshed. The revolution has, I think, already started. If it escalates, as well it might, the eyes of the world will be focused on the Republic, and relations, sporting and others, will be more difficult to maintain. The Lions in 1980 lent a helping hand. Those who received it will have to be more gracious and charitable internally in the near future, if friendships with the outside world are to be maintained.

I sympathize with the South Africans in their hour of need, but ultimately it is their problem, and only they can solve it.

Major tours usually provoke comment and discussion, so I shall conclude with these points:

1. The dropped goal should be reduced immediately to two points, to discourage its excessive use, and the penalty law needs a thorough overhaul.
2. Much of Beaumont's cleaning-up work of Colclough's deflections reminded me of the good old days of double banking.
3. The refereeing of the front rows in South Africa was deplorable, and exposed players to serious neck injuries. Collapsing of the scrummage is such a serious offence that I am delighted that the New Zealand Council has proposed that scrums should form in two stages, with front rows binding first, and then the other players joining them, so that the props and the hookers do not crash together with the full weight of the forwards behind them. I sincerely hope that the International Board will grant New Zealand a trial period for this important change of law.
4. I cannot offer any one reason for the large number of injuries suffered by the Lions. It certainly was not the result of violent play. Most of the matches, and all the Tests, were played in excellent spirit. It may have been a combination of hard grounds, the tackle law, the studs used by the Lions, insufficient exercise before sprinting, and muscle fatigue, but most probably, as I saw it, pure accidents, and very bad luck.
5. I do not like the presence of ball boys on the touchline. That the try scored by Germishuys was legal was due entirely to his presence of mind in making sure that he used the ball that was in play for the quick throw-in. Had he accepted a 'new' ball

from the ball boys, unnoticed by the referee, there might have been an international incident.

6. Neither do I like the presence of first-aiders. They are well-meaning people, but not always well enough trained to cope with a serious injury. Rodney O'Donnell could have been killed, had it not been for the presence of Dr John O'Driscoll on the field and Dr Jack Matthews on the touchline.

7. For continuity of treatment I am glad that the Lions took their own Medical Officer. For future tours I hope that they also take a qualified physiotherapist who is an authority on sports injuries.

Finally, congratulations to the Springboks and their selectors on winning the series. They played well, but not as well as they can. It was not a great series by any means.

Still there is plenty of talent in South Africa. A combination of the Test team and the best of the Junior Springboks and the Barbarians on a three-month overseas tour would work wonders for South African Rugby. The possibility of such a tour, however, is in the hands of the politicians!

Editor's Footnote

During my fascinating task the thought has constantly recurred, as I am sure it will to many readers, that the Lions, so often in so much trouble behind the scrum, had constantly with them one man who could have given them great help – Carwyn James. Yet he was never asked to do so. No one would suggest that the coach should have surrendered his authority; there was no need for that. Certainly Carwyn's assistance would have meant a change of tactics; it might also have meant victory.

R.C.   Chalfont St Peter, 1980

Appendix A
The 1980
British Lions

	Age	Height ft ins	Weight st lbs	Club	Caps
Manager					
Sydney Millar	45			Ballymena	37
Assistant Manager					
Noel Murphy	42			Cork Constitution	41
Captain					
W.B. Beaumont	28	6 3	16 0	Fylde	26
J.R. Beattie	22	6 3	15 0	Glasgow Academicals	4
P.J. Blakeway	29	5 10	16 7	Gloucester	4
S.O. Campbell	26	5 10	12 0	Old Belvedere	7
J. Carleton	24	5 10	13 0	Orrell	5
M.J. Colclough	26	6 5	17 6	Angoulême	6
F.E. Cotton	32	6 2	16 7	Sale	30
W.G. Davies	23	5 9	11 7	Cardiff	10
R.W.R. Gravell	28	5 11	13 12	Llanelli	18
B.H. Hay	30	5 10	13 7	Boroughmuir	17
T.D. Holmes	23	6 1	13 2	Cardiff	10
S.M. Lane	27	6 0	14 7	Cardiff	5
A.J. Martin	32	6 5	16 8	Aberavon	31
P. Morgan	21	5 10	12 5	Llanelli	2
R.C. O'Donnell	23	5 10	13 2	St Mary's College	5
J.B. O'Driscoll	26	6 2	15 2	London Irish	7
C.S. Patterson	25	5 5	11 0	Instonians	11
A.J. Phillips	24	5 11	14 4	Cardiff	5
G. Price	28	5 11	15 2	Pontypool	28
D.L. Quinnell	30	6 3	16 7	Llanelli	22
H.E. Rees	26	5 8	12 7	Neath	8
J.M. Renwick	28	5 8	12 7	Hawick	35

	Age	Height ft ins	Weight st lbs	Club	Caps
D.S. Richards	25	5 9	11 10	Swansea	6
M.A.C. Slemen	28	6 1	12 0	Liverpool	20
J. Squire	28	6 3	15 4	Pontypool	16
A.J. Tomes	28	6 6	18 0	Hawick	16
C.C. Tucker	27	6 1	15 2	Shannon	3
P.J. Wheeler	31	5 11	13 10	Leicester	24
C. Williams	31	6 0	15 8	Swansea	6
C.R. Woodward	24	5 11	12 7	Leicester	4
Replacements					
G. Williams	26	6 4	15 0	Bridgend	—
A.J.P. Ward	25	5 7	12 7	Garryowen	10
I. Stephens	28	5 10	16 0	Bridgend	—
J.C. Robbie	24	5 9	12 0	Greystones	5
P.A. Orr	29	5 10	15 10	Old Wesley	24
A.R. Irvine	28	5 10	12 10	Heriots F.P.	37
P.W. Dodge	23	6 2	12 10	Leicester	10
S.J. Smith	28	5 11	13 0	Sale	14

Appendix B
Appearances and Scorers

	Tests	Prov	T	PG	C	DG	Pts
Campbell	3	4	—	13	6	3	60
Woodward	2	9	4	8	5	1	53
Ward	1	4	1	11	4	1	48
Davies	1	3	1	7	3	1	34
Irvine	3	5	4	4	—	1	31
Slemen	1	4	5	—	1	1	25
Renwick	1	10	1	2	2	1	17
Holmes	—	4	3	—	—	—	12
Rees	—	6	3	—	—	—	12
Carleton	3	7	3	—	—	—	12
Quinnell	2	7	2	—	—	—	8
Price	4	8	2	—	—	—	8
Hay	3	8	2	—	—	—	8
O'Driscoll	4	7	2	—	—	—	8
Beattie	—	8	2	—	—	—	8
Robbie	1	6	1	—	—	1	7
Morgan	—	7	1	—	—	1	7
Wheeler	4	7	1	—	—	—	4
G. Williams	—	6	1	—	—	—	4
Richards	1	6	1	—	—	—	4
Patterson	3	7	1	—	—	—	4
Gravell	4	7	1	—	—	—	4
Dodge	2	3	1	—	—	—	4
Squire	4	7	1	—	—	—	4
Colclough	4	7	1	—	—	—	4
Tomes	—	7	1	—	—	—	4
C. Williams	4	8	1	—	—	—	4
O'Donnell	1	5	—	—	—	1	3
Beaumont	4	6					—
Tucker	2	7					—

	Tests	Prov	T	PG	C	DG	Pts
Cotton	—	4					—
Blakeway	—	1					—
Martin	—	8					—
Lane	—	1					—
Stephens	—	5					—
Orr	—	5					—
Phillips	—	7					—
Smith	—	—					—

Appendix C
The Players
in Person

Backs

RODNEY O'DONNELL, although talented and courageous, did not develop into the counter-attacking fullback that the Lions so badly needed. His line-kicking lacked distance, but no fault could be found with his tackling. It was a head-on tackle which caused the dislocation of his neck.

BRUCE HAY arrived on tour overweight and did not do himself justice, but his immense pluck, fearless tackling and experience enabled him to remain in the Test team. His combination with Andy Irvine eventually gave him the confidence he needed.

ANDY IRVINE looked a most inconsistent player, probably because he was never really fit. He could be brilliant, and yet he could make the most elementary mistakes. Despite an opening game of the highest quality, he never seemed entirely at peace with himself, but he was badly needed.

MIKE SLEMEN is an outstanding, mature footballer who could have played at Test level in any one of four positions. When he returned home after the first Test to be with his wife, who was having a difficult pregnancy, he had scored five tries, and he remained the Lions' top try-scorer to the end. There would have been many more tries for him during the six weeks he missed.

JOHN CARLETON was not the quickest of wings, which exposed him occasionally in both attack and defence, but he was surely one of the pluckiest players ever to wear a Lions' jersey. Having given up his job as a teacher to make the trip, he considered the sacrifice to have been well worth while.

ELGAN REES was let down too often by his catching. With the ball safely caught, he looked the fastest and most elusive of the wings. Like the other wings, he suffered from the disorganization in midfield, and he missed too many games because of injury: a rather sad tour for him.

PAUL DODGE is a safe centre and a strong runner who arrived as a replacement, and immediately won a Test place. This is probably a reflection on the original selection. He is a talented player who has yet to realize his full potential, but his presence did much to stiffen the Lions' midfield.

JIM RENWICK was robbed of a Lions' place three years previously when he was at his best, and in South Africa he was not the force on the field that he should have been, though he played well on occasions. He has a perceptive Rugby brain, and it is to be hoped that he will take up coaching.

RAY GRAVELL was the life and soul of the party, yet the most sensitive to criticism. He played the crash-ball game well, which was what the management wanted him to do, but he was prouder of his all too occasional outside break. By the third Test he was an important part of the Lions' tactical plan, but he needed constant reassurance from others that he was playing well.

DAVID RICHARDS is a gifted footballer who was better equipped in the kicking climate of South Africa to play in the centre. Having played average Rugby at outside-half in the earlier games, he then missed several games. On his return from his father's funeral, he was beginning to show brilliant form in the centre when he was too badly injured to continue.

CLIVE WOODWARD is a good handler and passer of the ball who proved to be the most elegant and exciting runner in the party, better on the wing than in the centre. He could beat an opponent more easily than most of his colleagues, and on his day he had a useful left foot. Had he been in the 1971 Lions' side, whose wings scored as many tries as the entire 1980 side, he might have become one of the greatest wing threequarters in the world.

PETER MORGAN was the baby of the party in years, but more gifted than most. He had to carry the utility tag. Utility players fill gaps, and on this tour there were few gaps for him to fill, yet one of the severest criticisms of the management is that they neglected him. His future in the game is probably brighter than anyone's.

Half-backs

GARETH DAVIES was in a class of his own. South Africa saw only briefly this younger version of Barry John. Of all the losses which the Lions suffered, the injury which forced Davies out of the tour was the most crucial. Had he played in the first Test the result of the match, and perhaps of the series, might have been different.

OLLIE CAMPBELL is a modest, charming young man, who played his game too seriously. He lacked joy and abandon. Instead of stretching for the ball and moving it, he would cradle it and caress it, and then, sensing the danger, he would have to kick it away. He tore a hamstring in the first week, and perhaps was not fully fit afterwards, for he could not repeat his record-breaking goal-kicking of a few months before.

TONY WARD suffered from the same fault as Campbell in that he did not get his threequarters moving at speed. His passing was cumbersome, and his running predictable, but his place-kicking was superb. He nearly won the first Test; had his tactical kicking been as good, the game would not have been lost.

TERRY HOLMES may not have been the best of the scrum-halves technically, but the other features of his game – his lethal breaks and his fearless tackling, which could match that of any flying flanker – were invaluable to a squad denied such an animal. It was a pity he was never in partnership with Gareth Davies in a Test match.

COLIN PATTERSON is a small player, but was extremely confident in his own ability. Technically this was considerable, but perhaps he was too confident. He went for five-metre breaks in the second and third Tests, and this may have cost the Lions a couple of victories. His luck ran out in the final week when his knee ligaments were severed, an injury which prevented his emigration to Australia.

JOHN ROBBIE deserved to play in the only successful Test. A fine technician, he had a wide vision of the game, gave his outside-halves a lot of space and time, and rarely took the wrong option. He is a natural leader, and it is to be hoped that he will be a candidate for the next Lions tour not only as scrum-half, but maybe also as captain.

Forwards

BILL BEAUMONT amply justified the selectors' faith. Anybody who thought the captaincy of the Lions in South Africa would be beyond the genial Lancastrian was quite wrong. He matured as a man as the tour went on, and there can have been few more popular captains. Tactically limited he may have been, but it was not his fault that he had no expert advice on back play. Without producing his usual storming loose play, he was most effective in the tight. Because of the Test record, posterity may not class him as an outstanding captain; those who travelled with him in 1980 know better.

FRAN COTTON, the great prop forward, was perhaps the most popular tourist of all, and the illness which forced him out of the tour had the most depressing effect on the rest of the party. Perhaps because he never felt one hundred per cent, he seemed unable to dominate opponents as he had done in the past.

CLIVE WILLIAMS was never mastered by any of the South African tight heads, and in the loose he was very much more mobile than he had been in New Zealand three years previously. Someone asked him how he liked the South African ball. 'How the hell would I know?' he replied, 'I never get a chance to touch the thing.' This was not to last, for he scored a try in the final Test.

IAN STEPHENS arrived as a replacement, like his Bridgend colleague Gareth Williams, and he took some time to settle down. Having done so, he played a sound game rather than a spectacular one.

PHIL ORR replaced Cotton and never seriously challenged Clive Williams for a Test place, but he certainly would not have let the side down if he had been called upon. He worked hard to dispel doubts about his fitness when he arrived, and became a valuable member of the tour party.

GRAHAM PRICE is a man of few words, but he is also the best tight-head prop in Rugby. South Africa had no one to compare with him, either in the tight or the loose. He was living proof of the adage that actions speak louder than words. At twenty-eight he has much yet to give to the game.

PHIL BLAKEWAY is a charming intelligent man, and as proud as anyone to be a Lion. Perhaps he ought not to have been allowed to go on the tour, because of his rib injury which was not examined after the Calcutta Cup match, but no blame can be attached to him. He took his disappointment at having to leave the tour with typical fortitude.

PETER WHEELER maintained his own incredibly high standard, set when he first got into the England side. Never outhooked, always sprightly in the loose, he had mastered every throw required in the modern lineout. Moreover the Lions could hardly have had a more conscientious or more efficient treasurer.

ALAN PHILLIPS was doomed, because of Wheeler's proficiency, to a secondary role, but he played it uncomplainingly. He trained hard, was always in readiness, and certainly would not have let the side down if he had been called upon for Test duty. He was an excellent tourist, and second only to Gravell as the team's humourist.

MAURICE COLCLOUGH was one of the outstanding successes of the tour. He realized his full potential, and finished as the heaviest man in the side at eighteen stone. He gave nothing away in the lineout, and his play in the tight was never matched by any South African lock.

ALAN TOMES, being the captain's understudy at lock, perhaps did not have the incentive to give of his best. Only against the Barbarians did he give a glimpse of the form he could attain. He was not helped by going on tour considerably overweight.

ALLAN MARTIN put a lot of work into the initial training period, and early in the tour seemed to be the man for the position of middle jumper for the Tests. However, Colclough played so well that Martin never had a chance to get into the Test side.

JOHN O'DRISCOLL was, with Colclough, the most improved player on the tour, and in fact the outstanding player in the party. His lack of pace was amply compensated for by his work-rate. It was due largely to O'Driscoll that Naas Botha's threat came to nothing. He was quite the best Lion in all four Tests.

COLM TUCKER was a surprise choice maybe, but he justified the selectors' faith. Not blessed with great pace, he made the most of his assets and was never far from play. He put an effective brake on Rob Louw in the third and fourth Tests.

JEFF SQUIRE began playing soundly without reaching his best, but his move to No. 8 for the last two Tests produced some fine Rugby from him. With O'Driscoll and Tucker he completed the Lions' best back row. It was his misfortune to have played in two dominant Lions packs and yet to have lost the Test series each time.

STUART LANE is perhaps the most unfortunate player ever to go on a Lions tour. He had fifty seconds of the first game before tearing the ligaments in his knee. His speed was sorely missed by the Lions. Like Blakeway he managed to make light of his disappointment and made the most of his tour until he had to go home.

DEREK QUINNELL began splendidly, and although he was given the captaincy of the midweek side he was clearly destined to be No. 8 in the Tests. After the second Test it was equally clear that more speed was needed in the back row, and Quinnell had to accept his role as midweek captain as the best he could attain.

JOHN BEATTIE is only twenty-two and lacks confidence in himself. His speed and his ability in the lineout were just what the Lions needed, but his lack of experience was all too obvious. Instead of going to work on him the management tended to ignore him. When he finally did tighten his game and become more belligerent, it was too late.

GARETH WILLIAMS was faster than the other flankers, but still lacked the pace of a Rob Louw. The Lions might have benefited from asking him to play as a specialized open-side flanker instead of playing left and right. Williams always looked good going forward, but less so in retreat.

STEVE SMITH is a very likeable lad from Sale who managed to cram more into his weekend excursion to South Africa than some of his colleagues did in ten weeks.

Appendix D
Match Details

Match 1

Eastern Province 16 pts,   British Lions 28
Played at Boet Erasmus, Port Elizabeth, on Saturday 10 May
Scorers: Eastern Province
> Tries: D. Campher, C. Heunis
> Penalty Goals: H. Pretorius, G. Cowley
> Conversion: G. Cowley
> *British Lions*
> Tries: E. Rees, M. Slemen, T. Holmes
> Penalty Goals: G. Davies (2), J. Renwick
> Conversions: G. Davies, J. Renwick
> Dropped goal: G. Davies

Eastern Province
H. Pretorius; H. Potgieter, H. Lotz, D. Campher, C. Heunis; G. Cowley, M. O'Shea; D. Oliver, K. Delport, J. Ferreira, A. Johnson, P. Human, S. Burger, T. van der Merwe (capt), N. Snyman.
> Replacements: G. van Zyl for Lotz; T. Kankowski for Potgieter.

British Lions
B. Hay; E. Rees, R. Gravell, P. Morgan, M. Slemen; G. Davies, T. Holmes; F. Cotton, P. Wheeler, G. Price, J. Squire, W. Beaumont (capt), A. Martin, S. Lane, J. Beattie.
> Replacements: J. Renwick for Davies; D. Quinnell for Lane.

Attendance: 30,000. Conditions: Dry, sunny, ground hard.
Referee: S. Strydom.

Match 2

SARA Invitation XV 6 pts,   British Lions 28
Played at East London on Wednesday 14 May
Scorers: SARA XV

>Penalty Goals: F. Prinsloo (2)
>*British Lions*
>Tries: D. Quinnell (2), E. Rees
>Penalty Goals: C. Woodward (3)
>Conversions: C. Woodward (2)
>Dropped Goal: C. Woodward

SARA XV
S. Mhlaba; T. Nkonki, H. Mhlaba, C. Eberson, S. Bridgeman; F. Prinsloo, W. Speelman; H. van Aswegen, E. Malan, C. Badenhorst, M. Cushe (capt), F. Weitz, A. Poro, T. McGee, T. Burger.

British Lions
R. O'Donnell; E. Rees, J. Renwick, C. Woodward, J. Carleton; D. Richards, C. Patterson; C. Williams, A. Phillips, P. Blakeway, C. Tucker, A. Tomes, M. Colclough, J. O'Driscoll, D. Quinnell (capt).
   Replacement: F. Cotton for Blakeway.

Attendance: 10,000. Conditions: Dry, sunny, ground hard.
Referee: J. Smith-Belton.

Match 3

Natal 15 pts,   British Lions 21
Played at King's Park, Durban, on Saturday 17 May
Scorers: Natal

>Try: Mortassagne
>Penalty Goals: C. Brown (3)
>Conversion: C. Brown
>*British Lions*
>Tries: J. Carleton, T. Holmes
>Penalty Goals: O. Campbell (2)
>Conversions: M. Slemen, O. Campbell
>Dropped Goal: M. Slemen

Natal
T. Cocks; L. Sharp, D. Hoffman, R. Haarhoff, C. Brown; P. Smith, P. Manning; M. Mortassagne, D. Speirs, B. de Klerk, M. Loane, A. Botha, H. van Heerden, W. Watt, W. Claassen (capt).

British Lions
R. O'Donnell; J. Carleton, R. Gravell, D. Richards, M. Slemen; O. Campbell,
T. Holmes; F. Cotton, P. Wheeler, G. Price, C. Tucker, W. Beaumont (capt),
A. Martin, J. Squire, J. Beattie.

Attendance: 40,000. Conditions: Dry, sunny, ground hard.
Referee: S. W. Malan.

Match 4

South African Invitation XV 19 pts,   British Lions 22
Played at Olenpark, Potchefstroom, on Wednesday 21 May
Scorers: S. A. Invitation XV
        Try: D. Smith
        Penalty Goals: R. Blair (5)
        British Lions
        Tries: M. Slemen (2)
        Penalty Goals: C. Woodward (4)
        Conversion: C. Woodward

S.A. Invitation XV
T. Cocks; T. Nkonki, D. Smith, H. Shields, N. Davids; R. Blair, D. Serfontein;
P. van der Merwe, W. Kahts, M. le Roux, J. Meyers, J. van Heerden, J. de
Villiers Visser, T. Burger, W. Claassen (capt).
  Replacement: T. Stofberg for Meyers.

British Lions
B. Hay; E. Rees, C. Woodward, J. Renwick, M. Slemen; D. Richards, C.
Patterson; C. Williams, A. Phillips, G. Price, J. O'Driscoll, A. Tomes, M.
Colclough, G. Williams, D. Quinnell (capt).

Attendance: 23,000. Conditions: Dry, ground hard.
Referee: G. Bezuidenhout.

Match 5

Orange Free State 17 pts,   British Lions 21
Played at Bloemfontein on Saturday 24 May
Scorers: Orange Free State
        Tries: D. Jeffrey, D. Gerber, B. Wolmarans
        Penalty Goal: G. Pienaar
        Conversion: G. Pienaar

British Lions
Tries: M. Slemen (2), T. Holmes, P. Wheeler
Penalty Goal: J. Renwick
Conversion: J. Renwick

Orange Free State
G. Pienaar; J. du Toit, D. Gerber, J. Rainsford, D. Jeffrey; de Wet Ras, B. Wolmarans (capt); D. Pretorius, K. Fenwick, M. le Roux, E. Jansen, J. Kritzinger, R. Visagie, J. Wessels, G. Sonnekus.
    Replacement: D. Froneman for de Wet Ras.

British Lions
P. Morgan; J. Carleton, R. Gravell, J. Renwick, M. Slemen; D. Richards, T. Holmes; C. Williams, P. Wheeler, G. Price, J. O'Driscoll, W. Beaumont (capt), M. Colcough, G. Williams, J. Squire.
    Replacement: C. Patterson for Holmes.

Attendance: 28,000. Conditions: Dry, sunny, ground hard.
Referee: F. Muller.

Match 6

South African Federation Invitation XV 6 pts   British Lions 15
Played at Danie Craven Stadium, Stellenbosch, on Tuesday 27 May
Scorers: Federation XV
    Penalty Goals: E. Tobias (2)
    British Lions
    Try: J. Carleton
    Penalty Goals: A. Ward (2)
    Conversion: A. Ward
    Dropped Goal: R. O'Donnell

Federation Invitation XV
R. Louw; J. Noble, C. Williams, H. Shields, F. Davids; E. Tobias, A. Lategan; H. van Aswegen, R. Cockrell, H. du Toit, K. Paarwater, J. de Villiers Visser, H. Bekker, W. Williams, P. Williams (capt).

British Lions
R. O'Donnell; J. Carleton, D. Richards, C. Woodward, P. Morgan; A. Ward, C. Patterson; F. Cotton, A. Phillips, I. Stephens, J. Beattie, A. Tomes, A. Martin, C. Tucker, D. Quinnell (capt).
    Replacement: C. Williams for Cotton.

Attendance: 10,000. Conditions: Dry, ground firm.
Referee: Dr G. Gouws.

Match 7 (The First Test)

SOUTH AFRICA 26 pts,   BRITISH ISLES 22
Played at Newlands, Cape Town, on Saturday 31 May
Scorers: South Africa
> Tries: J. Germishuys, W. du Plessis, D. Serfontein, R. Louw, J. van
> Heerden
> Conversions: N. Botha (3)
> *British Isles*
> Try: G. Price
> Penalty Goals: A. Ward (5)
> Dropped Goal: A. Ward

SOUTH AFRICA
G. Pienaar; R. Mordt, D. Smith, W. du Plessis, J. Germishuys; N. Botha, D.
Serfontein; R. Prentis, W. Kahts, M. le Roux, R. Louw, J. van Heerden, L.
Moolman, T. Stofberg, M. du Plessis (capt).

BRITISH ISLES
R. O'Donnell; J. Carleton, D. Richards, J. Renwick, M. Slemen; A. Ward, C.
Patterson; C. Williams, P. Wheeler, G. Price, J. Squire, W. Beaumont (capt),
M. Colclough, J. O'Driscoll, D. Quinnell.
  Replacement: R. Gravell for Carleton.

Attendance: 48,000. Conditions: Dry, sunny, ground firm.
Referee: F. Palmade.

Match 8

South African Country XV 7 pts,   British Lions 27
Played at Windhoek on Wednesday 4 June
Scorers: South African Country XV
> Try: C. Williams
> Penalty Goal: E. Tobias
> *British Lions*
> Tries: J. Renwick, C. Woodward, J. Beattie, G. Williams
> Penalty Goals: G. Davies (3)
> Conversion: G. Davies

South African Country XV
S. Mhlaba; E. Durrheim, J. Els, H. Shields, B. Venter; E. Tobias, F. Venter;
D. Mather, J. Volschenk, N. van Rensburg (capt), W. Wolfaardt, A. Botha, R.
Meier, M. Cushe, H. Shrader.
  Replacement: C. Williams for B. Venter.

British Lions
B. Hay (capt); C. Woodward, J. Renwick, R. Gravell, P. Morgan; G. Davies, J. Robbie; P. Orr, P. Wheeler, I. Stephens, C. Tucker, A. Tomes, A. Martin, G. Williams, J. Beattie.

Attendance: 9,000. Conditions: Dry, sunny, ground hard.
Referee: Col. N. Carstens.

Match 9

Transvaal 12 pts,   British Lions 32
Played at Wanderers' Ground, Johannesburg, on Saturday 7 June
Scorers: Transvaal
> Try: D. Maritz
> Penalty Goals: L. Barnard (2)
> Conversion: L. Barnard
> *British Lions*
> Tries: G. Davies, C. Patterson, D. Richards, C. Woodward (2), G. Price
> Penalty Goals: C. Woodward, A. Irvine
> Conversion: C. Woodward

Transvaal
P. Wilkinson; J. Fourie, W. Hollander, D. Maritz, J. Germishuys; L. Barnard, J. Minaar; R. Prentis, G. Venter, J. Strauss, C. Pypers (capt), K. de Klerk, L. van Vuren, T. Bosch, D. Macdonald.
  Replacement: B. Keevy for Wilkinson.

British Lions
A. Irvine; C. Woodward, R. Gravell, D. Richards, B. Hay; G. Davies, C. Patterson; P. Orr, P. Wheeler, G. Price, J. Squire, W. Beaumont (capt), M. Colclough, J. O'Driscoll, D. Quinnell.
  Replacement: J. Renwick for Richards.

Attendance: 35,000. Conditions: Dry, sunny, ground firm.
Referee: F. Burger.

Match 10

Eastern Transvaal 15 pts,   British Lions 21
Played at Springs on Tuesday 10 June
Scorers: Eastern Transvaal
> Penalty Goals: P. Geere (4)
> Dropped Goal: P. Geere

British Lions
Try: J. Carleton
Penalty Goals: O. Campbell (4)
Conversion: O. Campbell
Dropped Goal: O. Campbell

Eastern Transvaal
D. van Rensburg; L. Lubbe, J. Payne, E. Durrheim, C. van Zyl; P. Geere, P. Grobler; T. Botha, T. Kloppers, J. Volschenk, K. Fourie, K. van Wyk, K. Wentzel, M. van Eeden, W. Boshoff (capt).

British Lions
R. O'Donnell; J. Carleton, J. Renwick, P. Morgan, B. Hay (capt); O. Campbell, T. Holmes; C. Williams, A. Phillips, I. Stephens, C. Tucker, A. Tomes, A. Martin, G. Williams, J. Beattie.
   Replacement: C. Patterson for Holmes.

Attendance: 22,000. Conditions: Dry, sunny, ground hard.
Referee: J. Steenkamp.

Match 11 (The Second Test)

SOUTH AFRICA 26 pts,   BRITISH ISLES 19
Played at Bloemfontein on Saturday 14 June
Scorers: South Africa
   Tries: G. Pienaar, J. Germishuys, R. Louw, T. Stofberg
   Penalty Goals: N. Botha (2)
   Conversions: N. Botha (2)
   British Isles
   Tries: J. O'Driscoll, R. Gravell
   Penalty Goals: G. Davies (2), A. Irvine
   Conversion: G. Davies

SOUTH AFRICA
G. Pienaar; R. Mordt, D. Smith, W. du Plessis, J. Germishuys; N. Botha, D. Serfontein; R. Prentis, W. Kahts, M. le Roux, R. Louw, K. de Klerk, L. Moolman, T. Stofberg, M. du Plessis (capt).
   Replacement: T. Burger for Louw.

BRITISH ISLES
A. Irvine; J. Carleton, R. Gravell, C. Woodward, B. Hay; G. Davies, C. Patterson; C. Williams, P. Wheeler, G. Price, J. Squire, W. Beaumont (capt). M. Colclough, J. O'Driscoll, D. Quinnell.
   Replacement: O. Campbell for Davies.

Attendance: 60,000. Conditions: Dry, sunny, ground hard.
Referee: F. Palmade.

Match 12

Junior Springboks 6 pts,   *British Lions 17*
Played at Wanderers' Ground, Johannesburg, on Wednesday 18 June
Scorers: Junior Springboks
      Try: B. Geldenhys
      Conversion: G. Cowley.
      British Lions
      Tries: E. Rees, A. Irvine, P. Dodge
      Conversion: C. Woodward
      Dropped Goal: J. Renwick

Junior Springboks
T. Cocks; D. Botha, D. Gerber, C. Beck, D. Jeffrey; G. Cowley, G. Visagie;
J. Oberholtzer, E. Malan, H. du Toit, B. Geldenhys, J. de Villiers Visser, S.
Burger, E. Jansen, W. Claassen (capt).

British Lions
R. O'Donnell; E. Rees, J. Renwick, P. Dodge, A. Irvine; A Ward, J. Robbie;
P. Orr, A. Phillips, G. Price, J. Squire (capt), M. Colclough, A. Martin, J.
O'Driscoll, J. Beattie.
   Replacements: C. Woodward for O'Donnell, C. Williams for Orr.

Attendance: 35,000. Conditions: Dry, sunny, ground firm.
Referee: S. Strydom.

Match 13

Northern Transvaal 9 pts,   *British Lions 16*
Played at Loftus Versfeld, Pretoria, on Saturday 21 June
Scorers: Northern Transvaal
      Try: T. van der Merwe
      Conversion: N. Botha
      Dropped Goal: N. Botha
      British Lions
      Tries: M. Colclough, J. Squire
      Penalty Goals: A. Irvine (2)
      Conversion: O. Campbell

Northern Transvaal
P. Edwards; D. Botha, J. Knox, T. van der Merwe, P. van Zyl; N. Botha
(capt), T. du Plessis; J. Oberholtzer, W. Kahts, C. Badenhorst, B. Geldenhys,
T. Stofberg, L. Moolman, T. Burger, J. Marais.

British Lions
A. Irvine; C. Woodward, P. Dodge, R. Gravell, B. Hay; O. Campbell, J.
Robbie; C. Williams, P. Wheeler, G. Price, J. O'Driscoll, W. Beaumont (capt),
M. Colclough, C. Tucker, J. Squire.

Attendance 68,000. Conditions: Dry, sunny, ground hard.
Referee: Capt. F. Burger.

Match 14 (The Third Test)

SOUTH AFRICA 12 pts,   BRITISH ISLES 10
Played at Boet Erasmus Stadium, Port Elizabeth, on Saturday 28 June
Scorers: South Africa
> Try: J. Germishuys
> Penalty Goal: N. Botha
> Conversion: N. Botha
> Dropped Goal: N. Botha
> *British Isles*
> Try: B. Hay
> Penalty Goals: O. Campbell (2)

SOUTH AFRICA
G. Pienaar; R. Mordt, D. Smith, W. du Plessis, J. Germishuys; N. Botha, D.
Serfontein; R. Prentis, W. Kahts, M. le Roux, R. Louw, J. van Heerden, L.
Moolman, T. Stofberg, M. du Plessis (capt).
  Replacement: E. Malan for Kahts.

BRITISH ISLES
A. Irvine; C. Woodward, R. Gravell, P. Dodge, B. Hay; O. Campbell, C.
Patterson; C. Williams, P. Wheeler, G. Price, C. Tucker, W. Beaumont (capt),
M. Colclough, J. O'Driscoll, J. Squire.

Attendance: 40,000. Conditions: Wet, windy, ground soft.
Referee: J-P. Bonnet.

Match 15

South African Barbarians 14 pts,   British Lions 25
Played at King's Park, Durban, on Wednesday 2 July
Scorers: South African Barbarians
> Tries: F. Davids, I. Buchanan, M. Loane
> Conversion: H. Porta

British Lions
Tries: A. Tomes, A. Ward, A. Irvine
Penalty Goals: A. Ward (3)
Conversions: A. Ward (2)

S.A. Barbarians
S. Mhlaba; C. Williams, E. Tobias, P. Oosthuizen, F. Davids; H. Porta, I. Buchanan; M. Mortassagne, C. Rogers, T. Lupini, H. Meyers, A. Markgraaff, H. van Heerden, P. Fourie, M. Loane (capt).
Replacement: G. Visagie for Mhlaba.

British Lions
A. Irvine; E. Rees, J. Renwick, P. Morgan, J. Carleton; A. Ward, J. Robbie; P. Orr, A. Phillips, I. Stephens, D. Quinnell (capt), A. Tomes, A. Martin, G. Williams, J. Beattie.

Attendance: 30,000. Conditions: Dry, sunny, ground hard.
Referee: G. Harrison.

Match 16

Western Province 6 pts,   *British Lions 37*
Played at Newlands, Cape Town, on Saturday 5 July
Scorers: Western Province
Penalty Goals: C. Beck, D. Serfontein
British Lions
Tries: B. Hay, C. Woodward, A. Irvine
Penalty Goals: O. Campbell (4)
Conversions: O. Campbell (2)
Dropped Goals: O. Campbell (2), A. Irvine

Western Province
F. Naude; P. Oosthuizen, T. Eberson, W. du Plessis, P. Goosen; C. Beck, D. Serfontein; H. van Aswegen (capt), R. Cockrell, H. du Toit, R. Louw, J. de Villiers Visser, H. Bekker, D. Johnson, J. Geldenhys.

British Lions
A. Irvine; J. Carleton, R. Gravell, P. Dodge, B. Hay; O. Campbell, J. Robbie; C. Williams, P. Wheeler, G. Price, C. Tucker, W. Beaumont (capt), M. Colclough, J. O'Driscoll, J. Squire.
Replacement: C. Woodward for Irvine.

Attendance: 38,000. Conditions: Dry, sunny, ground firm.
Referee: F. Muller.

Match 17

Griqualand West 19 pts,   British Lions 23
Played at de Beers Stadium, Kimberley, on Tuesday 8 July
Scorers: Griqualand West
       Tries: T. Koch, P. Oosthuizen
       Penalty Goals: G. Visagie (3)
       Conversion: G. Visagie
       British Lions
       Tries: P. Morgan, J. Robbie, J. Beattie
       Penalty Goal: A. Ward
       Conversion: A. Ward
       Dropped Goals: P. Morgan, J. Robbie

Griqualand West
G. Rodwell; H. Lubbe, A. Gerber, J. Jooste, D. Prins; K. Erasmus, G. Visagie;
J. Harrison, B. O'Ehley, J. Brown, T. Koch, T. van Tonder, P. van Zyl (capt),
P. de Bruin, C. Oosthuizen.

British Lions
B. Hay; E. Rees, J. Renwick, C. Woodward, P. Morgan; A. Ward, C. Patterson;
P. Orr, A. Phillips, I. Stephens, G. Williams, A. Tomes, A. Martin, D. Quinnell
(capt), J. Beattie.
   Replacement: J. Robbie for Patterson.

Attendance 6,000. Conditions: Dry, sunny, ground hard.
Referee: Dr L. Wessels.

Match 18 (The Fourth Test)

SOUTH AFRICA 13 pts,   BRITISH ISLES 17
Played at Loftus Versfeld, Pretoria, on Saturday 12 July
Scorers: South Africa
       Try: W. du Plessis
       Penalty Goals: G. Pienaar (2), N. Botha
       British Isles
       Tries: C. Williams, A. Irvine, J. O'Driscoll
       Penalty Goal: O. Campbell
       Conversion: O. Campbell

SOUTH AFRICA
G. Pienaar; R. Mordt, D. Smith, W. du Plessis, J. Germishuys; N. Botha, D.
Serfontein; R. Prentis, E. Malan, M. le Roux, R. Louw, J. van Heerden, L.
Moolman, T. Stofberg, M. du Plessis (capt).

BRITISH ISLES
A. Irvine; J. Carleton, R. Gravell, P. Dodge, B. Hay; O. Campbell, J. Robbie;
C. Williams, P. Wheeler, G. Price, C. Tucker, W. Beaumont (capt), M.
Colclough, J. O'Driscoll, J. Squire.

Attendance: 68,000. Conditions: Dry, sunny, ground hard.
Referee: J-P. Bonnet.

	Played	Won	Drawn	Lost	Points for	Points against
Tests	4	1	0	3	68	77
Provincial	14	14	0	0	333	167
Total	18	15	0	3	401	244